CORNELIUS NEPOS
LIFE OF HANNIBAL

Cornelius Nepos
Life of Hannibal

Latin text, notes, maps,
illustrations and vocabulary

Bret Mulligan

OpenBook Publishers

http://www.openbookpublishers.com

© 2015 Bret Mulligan

The text of this work is licensed under a Creative Commons Attribution 4.0 International license (CC BY 4.0). This license allows you to share, copy, distribute and transmit the text; to adapt the text and to make commercial use of the text providing attribution is made to the author (but not in any way that suggests that he endorses you or your use of the work). Attribution should include the following information:

Bret Mulligan, *Cornelius Nepos, 'Life of Hannibal'. Latin Text, Notes, Maps, and Vocabulary*. Cambridge, UK: Open Book Publishers, 2015. http://dx.doi.org/10.11647/OBP.0068

Recordings © 2015 Christopher Francese

The recordings embedded in this volume are licensed under a Attribution-ShareAlike 4.0 International license (CC BY-SA 4.0). This means that if you remix, transform, or build upon the recordings, you must distribute your contributions under the same license.

Further details about CC licenses are available at http://creativecommons.org/licenses/

Please see the list of illustrations for attribution relating to individual images. Every effort has been made to identify and contact copyright holders and any omission or error will be corrected if notification is made to the publisher. For information about the rights of the Wikimedia Commons images, please refer to the Wikimedia website (the relevant links are listed in the list of illustrations).

In order to access detailed and updated information on the license, please visit http://www.openbookpublishers.com/isbn/9781783741328#copyright

All external links were active on 25/09/2015 unless otherwise stated.

Digital material and resources associated with this volume are available at http://www.openbookpublishers.com/isbn/9781783741328#resources. Mulligan's commentary is also available online at http://dcc.dickinson.edu/nepos-hannibal/preface

ISBN Paperback: 978-1-78374-132-8
ISBN Hardback: 978-1-78374-133-5
ISBN Digital (PDF): 978-1-78374-134-2
ISBN Digital ebook (epub): 978-1-78374-135-9
ISBN Digital ebook (mobi): 978-1-78374-136-6
DOI: 10.11647/OBP.0068

Cover image: Sébastien Slodtz, *Hannibal Barca Counting the Rings of the Roman Knights Killed at the Battle of Cannae in 216 BC* (1704). http://commons.wikimedia.org/wiki/File:Hannibal_Slodtz_Louvre_MR2093.jpg

All paper used by Open Book Publishers is SFI (Sustainable Forestry Initiative), PEFC (Programme for the Endorsement of Forest Certification Schemes) and Forest Stewardship Council(r)(FSC(r) certified.

Printed in the United Kingdom and United States by Lightning Source
for Open Book Publishers (Cambridge, UK).

Contents

Preface	vii
Acknowledgements	ix
List of Illustrations	xi
1. Life of Nepos	**1**
Historical Context	2
Works of Nepos	3
The Lives of Famous Men	4
The Lives of Foreign Commanders	4
Other Works	5
Reputation in Antiquity and Beyond	6
Friendships & Social Context	8
The Caecilii Metelli	8
Atticus & Cicero	9
Catullus	11
2. Reading Nepos	**13**
Four Favorite Constructions	14
Three Key Words	15
Why Write Biography?	15
Nepos and Non–Roman Cultures	17
The Biographical Tradition in Greece and Rome	17
Nepos' Audience	19
3. Historical Context and Hannibal	**21**
Early History of Carthage	21
First Punic War (264–241 BC)	24
Between the Wars	28
Second Punic War (218–201 BC)	29
Aftermath	35
Hannibal	37
Evaluating Hannibal	41

Bibliography 43
Chronology of Hannibal's Life 47

Text of Nepos' *Life of Hannibal* 51
   Prologus 51
   Chapter 1 52
   Chapter 2 53
   Chapter 3 54
   Chapter 4 54
   Chapter 5 55
   Chapter 6 56
   Chapter 7 56
   Chapter 8 57
   Chapter 9 58
   Chapter 10 59
   Chapter 11 60
   Chapter 12 61
   Chapter 13 62

Notes 63
   Prologus 63
   Essay on Nepos' *Prologus* to the *Lives of Outstanding Commanders* 68
   Chapter 1 69
   Chapter 2 73
   Chapter 3 80
   Chapter 4 84
   Essay on The Battle of Cannae & Its Legacy 87
   Chapter 5 89
   The End of Hannibal's Campaign in Italy (218–203 BC) 94
   Chapter 6 95
   Chapter 7 98
   Chapter 8 104
   Chapter 9 107
   Chapter 10 110
   Chapter 11 113
   Chapter 12 117
   Chapter 13 121

Full Vocabulary for Nepos' *Life of Hannibal* and *Prologus* to the *Lives of Outstanding Commanders* 123

Preface

This book contains the Latin text, notes, and vocabulary for Cornelius Nepos' *Life of Hannibal*. It also includes the *Prologus* (*Preface*) to Nepos' biographies of foreign commanders. Although the *Prologus* is not essential for understanding the *Life of Hannibal*, it does provide valuable insight into why Nepos wrote biography and how he understood the relationship between Roman and non–Roman values.

As Rome completed its bloody transition from dysfunctional republic to (mostly) stable monarchy, Cornelius Nepos (ca. 100–27 BC) labored to complete an innovative and influential collection of concise biographies. Putting aside the detailed, chronological accounts of military campaigns and political machinations that characterized most writing about history, Nepos surveyed Roman and Greek history for distinguished men who excelled in a range of prestigious occupations. In the exploits and achievements of these illustrious men, Nepos hoped that his readers would find models for the honorable conduct of their own lives.

Although most of Nepos' works have been lost, we are fortunate to have his biography of the Carthaginian general Hannibal. One of history's most celebrated military leaders, Hannibal waged a brilliant—if ultimately futile—campaign against Rome during the Second Punic War (218–202 BC). Nepos sketches Hannibal's life from the time he began traveling with his father's army as a young boy, through his sixteen–year invasion of Italy and his tumultuous political career in Carthage, to his perilous exile and eventual suicide far from Carthage. Nepos' biography offers a surprisingly balanced portrayal of a man that many Roman authors vilified as the most monstrous foe that Rome had ever faced.

Nepos' preference for common vocabulary, his relatively straightforward style, and the historical interest of the material make this text suitable for those who are beginning to read continuous Latin prose. Attention is paid throughout this commentary to how Nepos constructs his sentences and how he combines these sentences into a continuous narrative. Each chapter features a running list of the (relatively few) words that are not found in the Dickinson College Commentaries Latin Core available at http://dcc.dickinson.edu/latin-vocabulary-list. To help readers acquaint themselves with the events of Hannibal's lifetime, historical notes and explanations of Roman and Carthaginian culture are frequent. Customizable vocabulary lists for this text are available at http://bridge.haverford.edu

Acknowledgements

I would like to extend my abiding thanks to my colleagues at Haverford College for their support, in particular Sydnor Roy, who allowed me to eavesdrop on her Elementary Latin students as they used this commentary. Instructors too numerous to thank by name have made suggestions and caught errors. Students in Latin classes at Wheaton College and Haverford College made suggestions on early versions of the commentary and proved by experience those aspects of Nepos' text that needed clarification. Haverford students Florencia Foxley, Eliana Kohrman–Glaser, Carman Romano, Emma Mongoven, and Hannah Silverblank made significant contributions to editing the commentary, as well as developing vocabulary lists and other supplemental resources. Laurie Allen (Coordinator for Digital Scholarship and Services), Michael Zarafonetis (Digital Scholarship Librarian), Margaret Schaus (Lead Research and Instruction Librarian), and Julie Coy (Visual Resources Librarian) contributed indispensable expertise throughout. Support for the development of this book was provided by Haverford's Office of the Provost and the John B. Hurford '60 Center for the Arts and Humanities.

Maps were adapted from Map Tiles, Ancient World Mapping Center © 2015 (http://awmc.unc.edu). Used by permission.

This printable edition has been adapted from the digital edition prepared for the Dickinson College Commentaries Series which is freely available online at http://dcc.dickinson.edu

The Latin texts of Nepos' *Preface* and the *Life of Hannibal* are based on that of J. C. Rolfe's Loeb edition (1929). In addition to minor alterations to the punctuation of the text, two changes have been made in accordance with the judgment of Marshall 1977: in 4.3 *nimium* is read for *etiam tum;* and in 9.3 *omnēs suā pecūniā* for *omnī suā pecūniā*. To avoid unnecessary confusion, *servulīs* is read for *servolīs* in 8.2 and *Prūsias* is read for the analogous *Prūsia* in 12.3. Macrons have been added to the text in accordance with the quantities found in the *Woordenboek Latijn/Nederlands* (2011, 5th revised edition).

Bret Mulligan, Haverford College, May 2015

List of Illustrations

1. Map of Northern Italy. Adapted with permission from images © Ancient World Mapping Center, CC BY-NC-ND. http://awmc.unc.edu/wordpress/alacarte/ — xii
2. Carthaginian and Roman territory on the eve of the First Punic War. Adapted with permission from images © Ancient World Mapping Center, CC BY-NC-ND. — 22
3. *Dido Building, Carthage* (1815) by J. M. W. Turner. Oil on canvas. 155.5x232 cm. Now at the National Gallery, London. Wikimedia, https://commons.wikimedia.org/wiki/File:Turner_-_Dido.jpg — 22
4. Hannibal's route into Italy. Adapted with permission from images © Ancient World Mapping Center, CC BY-NC-ND. — 30
5. *Snow Storm, Hannibal and his Army Crossing the Alps* (1810–1812) by J. M. W. Turner. Oil on canvas. 144.7x236 cm. Now at Tate Britain, London. Wikimedia, https://commons.wikimedia.org/wiki/File:Joseph_Mallord_William_Turner_081.jpg — 31
6. Hannibal's campaign in Italy. Adapted with permission from images © Ancient World Mapping Center, CC BY-NC-ND. — 33
7. *The Capture of Carthage* (1539). Engraving by George Pencz. Now at the Los Angeles County Museum of Art. Wikimedia, https://commons.wikimedia.org/wiki/File:Georg_Pencz_-_The_Capture_of_Carthage.jpg — 36
8. Roman bust of Hannibal. Statue in marble. Capua, Italy. Now at the Museo Archeologico Nazionale, Naples. Wikimedia, https://commons.wikimedia.org/wiki/File:Mommsen_p265.jpg — 38
9. Hannibal's travels in the East (196–183 BC). Adapted with permission from images © Ancient World Mapping Center, CC BY-NC-ND. — 40
10. Hannibal's Oath of Hatred Against Rome. Drawing by Joelle Cicak, CC BY. — 77
11. Hannibal's Ruse of the Amphorae. Drawing by Joelle Cicak, CC BY. — 108
12. Snakes on a Boat. Drawing by Joelle Cicak, CC BY. — 112
13. Hannibal Surrounded. Drawing by Joelle Cicak, CC BY. — 119

1. Map of Northern Italy.

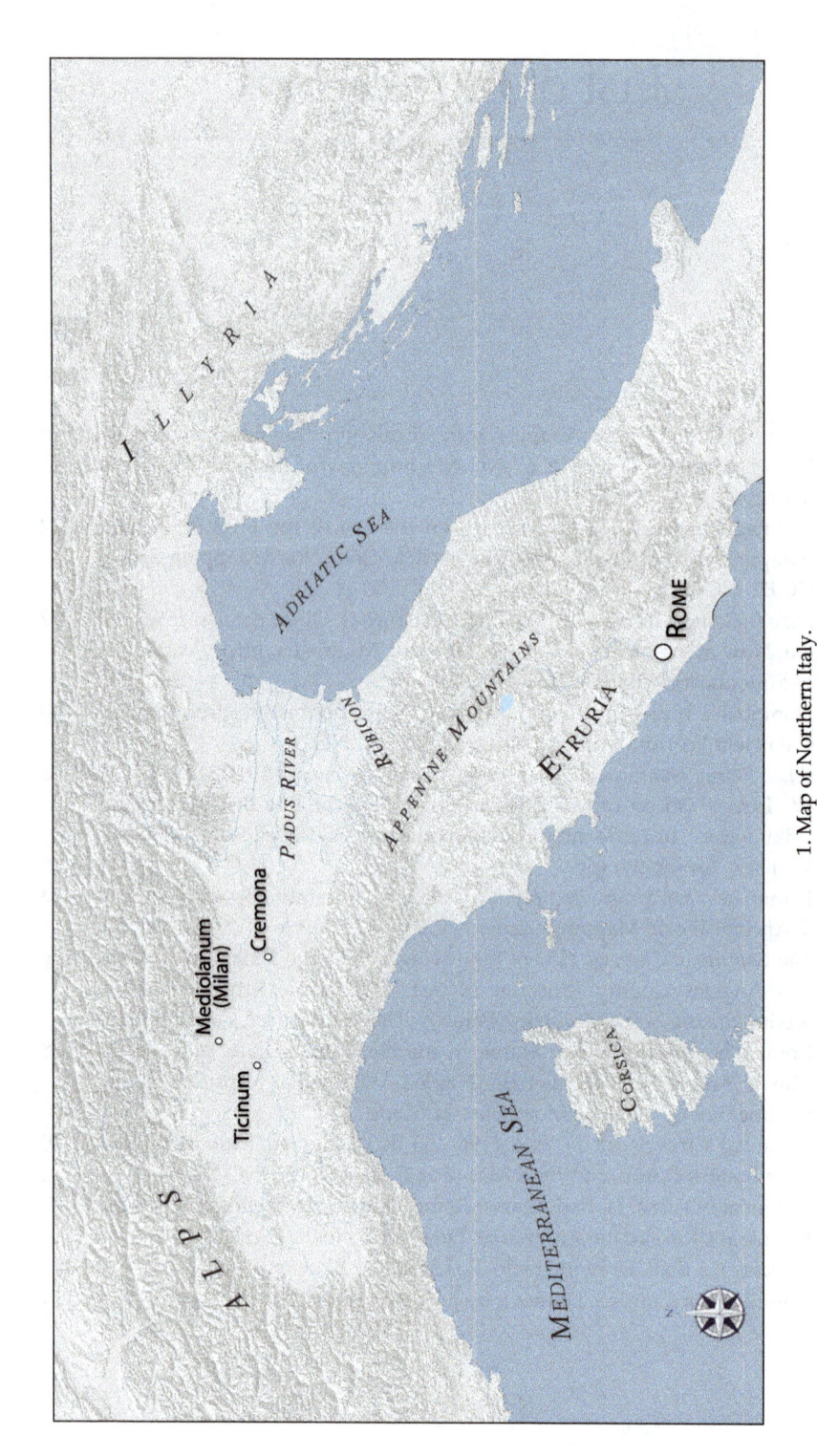

Adapted with permission from images © Ancient World Mapping Center, CC BY-NC-ND. http://awmc.unc.edu/wordpress/alacarte/

1. Life of Nepos

For a man who devoted such energy to chronicling the exploits of famous men, Cornelius Nepos left behind few clues about his own life. Nepos was likely born within a decade of 100 BC in Cisalpine Gaul, the district of northern Italy bounded to the north by the Alps and to the south by the Rubicon River. This prosperous region would produce many of the great Roman authors, including Catullus, Virgil, Livy, Pliny the Elder, and his nephew Pliny the Younger. Nepos' hometown is unknown, but Ticinum and Mediolanum are plausible candidates.

We can be sure that Nepos was not a member of the senatorial elite.[1] Nevertheless, Nepos' family possessed sufficient wealth to finance his education and then support his academic pursuits in Rome. He may have immigrated to Rome—Nepos comments on how Roman fashions changed after Sulla gained power in the late 80s.[2] He had certainly arrived in the city by 65 BC, in time to hear Cicero defend the former tribune C. Cornelius against charges of sedition.[3] Rome was likely his home for the remainder of his life, although, like many affluent Romans, Nepos travelled—to Greece, Asia Minor, and North Africa, and perhaps even further afield. Nepos died soon after 27 BC, in the early years of Augustus' reign.[4]

---

1 Pliny the Younger, *Epistles* 5.3.6.
2 Pliny the Elder, *Natural History* 4.28.
3 Jerome, *Against John of Jerusalem* 12.
4 Pliny the Elder, *Natural History* 9.137 and 10.60.

© Bret Mulligan, CC BY 4.0 http://dx.doi.org/10.11647/OBP.0068.01

Historical Context

Nepos lived during the tumultuous final years of the Roman republic. He was likely born in the closing decade of the second century BC, within a few years of Atticus (110 BC), Catiline (108 BC), Cicero and Pompey (106 BC), and Caesar (100 BC). Around this same time, migrating Germanic tribes repeatedly defeated Roman armies and even threatened northern Italy with invasion (113–101 BC). To confront this peril, the consul Marius transformed the Roman army into a permanent and professional force open to all Roman citizens, a development that decisively resolved the manpower crisis that had constrained Roman military power since the Punic Wars, but which contributed to no small amount of mischief and sorrow over the subsequent eighty years, as generals supported by armies of loyal veterans tore the Roman republic apart.

When Nepos was still a child, Rome experienced the twin traumas of the Social War (91–88 BC)—a vicious conflict resolved only when Rome's Italian allies were granted full citizenship rights—and the chaos of the 80s, when a series of rival Roman generals occupied Rome and political power was wielded at sword point. It was likely soon after Spartacus' slave revolt (73–71 BC) that Nepos arrived in Rome. There he would have witnessed Cicero's suppression of the Catilinarian conspiracy (64–63 BC) and the consequent recriminations that led to Cicero's exile (58–56 BC). Nepos lived in Rome for much of the next four decades, witnessing the ascendency of Pompey (67–49 BC), Caesar's triumph in the civil war and his eventual assassination (49–44 BC), the uneasy peace between Octavian and Marcus Antonius in the 30s, and, finally, Octavian's consolidation of power after his victory at the Battle of Actium in 31 BC.

Apart from a few isolated jabs at disreputable figures like Spinther and Mamurra, Nepos seems to inhabit a world apart from the epochal events that he must have witnessed—a man in but not of his time. He may as well have been speaking of himself when he praises Atticus' cautious neutrality:

> He did not mingle in civil tumults, because he thought that those who had plunged into them were not more under their own control than those who were tossed by the waves of the sea.[5]

Nevertheless, some hints of Nepos' views on the changing political landscape of the late republic emerge from his *Lives*. His biographies

---

5   Nepos, *Life of Atticus* 6.1

display a systematic interest in how events can make and unmake a state. Nepos often emphasizes the importance of obedience to the state over personal ambition and how the decisions made by leaders can contribute to peace or bring about civic disaster. Throughout his works, men are praised for striving to preserve the difficult work of liberty in the face of the temptations of tyranny. It is not difficult to see these themes as implicit commentary on the behavior of Caesar, Brutus, Cicero, Antonius, and Octavian.

A comment in his *Life of Eumenes* indicates that Nepos was a keen observer of the troubles that gripped Rome during this period. As he reflected on the conquests of Alexander the Great, Nepos observed how success had induced Alexander's Macedonian soldiers to "claim the right to command its leaders instead of obeying them".[6] Nepos perceived the same troubling loss of discipline among Rome's veterans, who he feared would "ruin everything by their intemperance and excessive licentiousness, both those that they support and those that they fight".[7] If we could read his letters or his biographies on politically active Romans, we would doubtless have a better sense of how Nepos understood the transformation of Roman politics and culture during his lifetime; his *Life of Cicero* would likely be especially telling in this regard. In their absence, our impression of Nepos remains that of a dedicated scholar, a man who, like his friend Atticus, socialized with the movers and shakers of his day, but remained aloof from the murderous politics of the late republic.

Works of Nepos

Like Atticus, Varro, and the other Roman polymaths who lived during the late republic, Nepos was a prolific author who wrote in many genres. In addition to his collection of biographies, he composed poetry and wrote works on history, geography, and rhetoric. Nepos is credited with several literary "firsts". One of these arose by chance: he is the first biographer from Classical antiquity—Greek or Latin—from whom a complete biography survives. Although he did not invent the genre, Nepos did introduce political biography of Greek statesmen to a Roman audience. Nepos appears to have been the first author to attempt a systematic

---

6 Nepos, *Life of Eumenes* 8.2–3.
7 Ibid., 8.3.

collection of biographies across a range of professions. Nepos' account of the life of his friend Atticus may have been the first biography written about a living contemporary and is the only surviving Latin biography about an *eques*—a member of Rome's commercial class. Nepos was also the first Roman to attempt to synchronize Italian history with the mature tradition of Greek historiography—an audacious feat that elicited generous praise from the discriminating poet Catullus. Accustomed as we are today to a standardized, international chronological system, it is difficult to appreciate Nepos' achievement in this area, which required him to synthesize events recorded in numerous conflicting and discontinuous calendrical systems maintained by individual cities around the Mediterranean.

The Lives of Famous Men

Nepos' most ambitious project was *The Lives of Famous Men* (*De viris illustribus*), most of which is now lost. This collection of biographies likely included sixteen books divided into eight thematic pairs. The first book of each pair contained biographies of non–Romans, for the most part Greeks, who were preeminent in a particular profession. The next book of each pair presented the lives of exceptional Romans in the same field. Nepos certainly produced volumes containing the biographies of commanders and historians. We can be reasonably confident that Nepos also composed biographies of philosophers, poets, and orators, among other professionals. All told, the *Lives* once contained hundreds of biographies—a work of scholarship that was spectacular and sweeping, if not without its faults.

The Lives of Foreign Commanders

Only one book of Nepos' *Lives* has survived: his biographies of foreign commanders. Nepos dedicated this book to his close friend Atticus, who could well have encouraged Nepos to undertake this grand comparative project. Nepos published the first edition of the *Lives*, which included the biographies of nineteen Greek commanders arranged in rough chronological order, a few years before Atticus passed away in 32 BC. The lives of three non–Greek commanders—those of Hannibal, his father Hamilcar, and the Persian general Datames—may have been added in a second edition published sometime before 27 BC.

In its current form, *The Lives of Foreign Commanders* displays several unusual features that suggest that Nepos may not have published this book of *Lives* in the exact form that we now possess. Taken together, these twenty-two biographies would represent one of the longest books to survive from antiquity. In addition to the atypical length of the book, we must account for the clipped nature of Nepos' style and the not infrequent errors and often vexing omissions that pepper the biographies—failings that are utterly at odds with Nepos' reputation in antiquity. These features could suggest that the *Lives* were altered, perhaps extensively, after Nepos' death.

When might such alterations have occurred? As the Classical world transitioned into the Middle Ages, many works, especially those of considerable length like Nepos' collected *Lives*, were shortened, epitomized, or otherwise simplified. It seems almost certain that Nepos' work was subjected to extensive editing and manipulation during this period. Some of the longer *Lives* may have been condensed; the *Life of Aristides* and a few others may even have been forged at this time. Indeed, it was a misunderstanding related to this editorial process that resulted in the *Lives* being misattributed during the Middle Ages to a late antique copyist (and minor poet) by the name Aemilius Probus. It was only in the sixteenth century that Nepos reclaimed his status as the genuine author of the *Lives*.

The challenges posed by a redacted text like the *Lives* serve as a powerful reminder of the complex journey undertaken by almost every text that survives from antiquity. Apart from those few works that survive in ancient inscriptions or on papyri, most works of Classical antiquity are products of a perilous, often haphazard transmission from antiquity to modernity. Although written by Nepos, the *Lives* passed through the innumerable hands of copyists, editors, redactors, and scholars until they reached the form that we read today. At one point in the twelfth century, Nepos survived in only a single manuscript—that was how close Nepos came to oblivion. While we can and should ponder what has been lost and altered in the process, we can also marvel at the millennial undertaking that preserved (often just barely) the works of antiquity for readers in the modern age.

Other Works

Apart from *The Lives of Foreign Commanders*, only two complete works survive from Nepos' voluminous writings: an innovative biography of his friend and contemporary Atticus (his longest biography) and a very concise summary of his biography of Cato the Elder, which was written at

Atticus' request. Excerpts of a letter from Cornelia, the mother of Tiberius and Gaius Gracchus, were transmitted with Nepos' works. It is unclear if Nepos himself quoted these excerpts in a now lost work or if they were simply appended to Nepos' works at some point by a later scribe.

In addition to the *Lives*, Nepos composed several other works, now lost:

- Extensive biographies of Cato the Elder and Cicero in two books. A redacted version of the biography of Cato survives; Gellius mentions the biography of Cicero.[8]
- Correspondence with Cicero, and we might assume other notable contemporaries.
- The *Chronica* (*Chronicle*), a chronology in three books. The first work of Roman historiography not concerned exclusively with Roman or Italian history, it sought to synchronize the histories of Rome, Greece, and the Near East from the dawn of humanity down to Nepos' time. Catullus' knowledge of the work indicates that it must have been published before the poet's death (ca. 54 BC), and probably some years earlier. Despite Catullus' praise, the *Chronica* was soon eclipsed by Atticus' more succinct *Liber annalis* (published in 47 BC; also lost).
- The *Exempla* (*Models*), a compendium of moralizing historical anecdotes in at least five books, published after 43 BC.[9] Designed to serve as a reference guide for orators and authors, it was perhaps the first work of its kind and was much imitated. Of Nepos' works it was the most frequently cited in antiquity.
- A treatise on geography, perhaps focused on the periphery of Europe and those areas settled by the Celts.[10]
- A mysterious treatise on literary terminology, which included a discussion about *literati*, scholars who interpreted the works of poets.[11]
- Love poems, perhaps in the neoteric style favored by Catullus and his friends. Pliny the Younger mentions Nepos' poetry and his sterling character in a defense of his own decision to compose light poetry.[12]

Reputation in Antiquity and Beyond

Nepos was well-respected as a historian and biographer throughout antiquity, and a hundred years after his death Pliny the Younger would rank Nepos as one of the most distinguished men from his hometown

---

8   Aulus Gellius, *Attic Nights* 15.28.2.
9   Charisius, *Ars Grammatica*, I 146K; Aulus Gellius, 6.18.11.
10 Pliny the Elder, *Natural History* 3.4, 3.132, 4.77.
11 Suetonius, *De grammaticis* 4.
12 Pliny the Younger, *Letters* 5.3.6.

(wherever it was).[13] The geographer Pomponius Mela cites Nepos as an authority for his assertion that the entire world was surrounded by ocean.[14] Pliny the Elder believed he was a reliable source on geography from North Africa to Asia Minor to the Caspian Sea and preferred him to many other sources, although he also cautioned that Nepos was prone to believing fantastic stories.[15] Pliny the Younger placed Nepos in the illustrious company of Ennius, the tragedian Accius, and Virgil as great authors who hailed from humble backgrounds.[16] In late antiquity, Jerome would describe Nepos as "a famous writer of history" and "the most notable biographer".[17]

Nepos long retained his reputation as an authoritative scholar. In the fifth or sixth century AD, an anonymous author began circulating a forged "true history" of the Trojan War. This forgery, *The History of the Fall of Troy*, purported to be an eyewitness account of the war by Dares, a minor Trojan priest mentioned in passing by Homer. Before the start of the *History*, the forger affixed a letter by "Nepos" to his friend, the historian Sallust. In this forged letter, "Nepos" claims to have rediscovered Dares' work while conducting research in Athens. He immediately made "an exact translation into Latin, neither adding nor omitting anything, nor giving any personal touch" and forwarded his "word for word" translation to Sallust. The use of Nepos' name to legitimize this forgery speaks to the authority that he continued to have as a scholar and researcher even in the waning decades of Classical antiquity.

Although the Romans admired Nepos for his wit, knowledge, and aesthetic judgment, many modern scholars have found fault with his *Lives*. What can explain the gap between his ancient reputation as a sophisticated author and the repetitive style—and not infrequent errors, omissions, and other blunders—that modern readers have detected in his work? First, we should remember that Nepos' Lives were not works of original scholarship. Rather, they drew almost exclusively from previous sources for their information regarding historical figures. He did not aim to discover an accurate portrayal of historical truth, nor was he attempting to produce definitive and exhaustive biographies of his subjects. Nepos aimed instead to provide biographical sketches that revealed higher truths and eternal

---

13 *Ibid.*, 4.28.
14 Pomponius Mela, 3.44.
15 Pliny the Elder, *Natural History* 5.4.
16 Pliny the Younger, *Letters* 5.3.6.
17 Jerome, *Chronicle* 1977.

virtues. This is not to dismiss those errors that are present; but these should be assessed in light of Nepos' goals and interests in undertaking his biographical project. Second, we should recognize that Nepos has been ill-served by the section of the *Lives* that happened to survive. Of all his biographies, the exploits of foreign generals stood the furthest from his own training and personal experiences. Had the lost books detailing the more familiar lives of the Roman generals or those on Roman poets or orators survived, we might well have a different opinion of Nepos' accuracy and judgment.

Friendships & Social Context

In Rome, Nepos devoted himself to his studies, avoiding the increasingly dangerous politics of the late republic. He forged durable friendships with several famous Romans: the politician Metellus Celer, the scholar Atticus, the statesman Cicero, and the poet Catullus. These relationships provide glimpses into Nepos' life, as well as valuable information about the intellectual context for his writings.

The Caecilii Metelli

There is indirect evidence that Nepos enjoyed a close relationship with the Caecilii Metelli, one of the wealthiest and most influential families in Rome. Nepos' writings often display a special interest in commemorating the achievements of members of this family. And on several occasions Nepos maligned the decadent luxury of one of the family's notorious political rivals: Publius Cornelius Lentulus Spinther. From the historian Pomponius Mela we learn that Nepos was a personal acquaintance of Metellus Celer, brother to Metellus Nepos and husband of the notorious Clodia (the lover of Catullus). According to Mela, Metellus Celer once told Nepos about the fantastic sea voyage endured by a group of Indian merchants. Carried all the way to northern Europe by a terrible storm, the Indians were captured by a local German chieftain, who then presented them as a gift to Celer.[18] Nepos may have been a client of this powerful family, or his intellectual pursuits may have led to a more equal friendship with Celer. Regardless of the exact nature of their relationship, his association with this powerful family demonstrates Nepos' access to the upper echelons of Roman society.

---

18   Pomponius Mela, 3.44.

Atticus & Cicero

Soon after arriving in Rome, Nepos forged a lasting friendship with Titus Pomponius Atticus (ca. 109–ca. 32 BC), the adopted son of Quintus Caecilius Metellus. Atticus was a close friend of Cicero and a distinguished patron of the literary arts in Rome. Nepos would compose a laudatory biography of Atticus (the longest of his works to survive) and dedicate several works to his friend, including the book of biographies that contains the *Life of Hannibal*. Atticus, who often goaded Cicero to attempt writing in new literary genres, convinced Nepos to write his *Life of Cato* and may likewise have encouraged Nepos to begin work on his innovative project of comparative biography.

It may have been through Atticus that Nepos met Cicero, Rome's greatest orator. Like Nepos, Cicero had immigrated to Rome as a young man from a small Italian town. But unlike Nepos, Cicero had devoted himself to politics, becoming one of the central figures in the contentious partisan drama of the late republic. Despite their different dispositions, Nepos became one of Cicero's more frequent correspondents—two books of letters from Cicero to Nepos were known in antiquity, although these are now lost.[19] According to Aulus Gellius (ca. AD 125–180), Nepos was "one of Cicero's most intimate friends" (*maxime amicus familiaris*).[20] Other evidence, however, points to a relationship that was more cordial than close.

Disagreement about the value of philosophy seems to have contributed to the tension between Cicero and Nepos. In 44 BC, when Atticus mentioned that Nepos was eager to read Cicero's latest philosophical work, Cicero expressed his doubts about Nepos' sincerity, since Nepos had previously disparaged Cicero's philosophical works as merely a venue in which he could "display his pride".[21] While Cicero sought solace and wisdom from philosophy in the final years of his life, Nepos was skeptical that philosophy could be an "instructor of life" (*magistram vitae*). Nepos observed that the same philosophers who taught "most cunningly in the school about modesty and continence" were often those who lived the most hedonistic lives of luxury.[22] For Nepos, good character was cultivated by observing and emulating virtuous behavior, not by abstract philosophizing.

---

19 Macrobius, *Saturnalia* 2.1.14; Suetonius, *Julius* 55.
20 Aulus Gellius, 15.28.2.
21 Cicero, *Letters to Atticus* 16.5.5.
22 Nepos' criticisms of Cicero's philosophical works were preserved by Christian authors who were always on the lookout for anecdotes that exposed the hypocrisy of pagan

Nepos' friendship with Cicero illustrates the difficulties we face in attempting to reconstruct the life of the biographer. Since Cicero's letters to Nepos have not survived, our best evidence about their relationship comes from passing comments that Cicero made to Atticus, who often acted as an intermediary between his two friends. For example, it was Atticus who informed Cicero that Nepos' young son had passed away in 44 BC. Cicero expresses his sadness at Nepos' loss, but also, in an obscure passage, claims that he was unaware of the child's existence.[23] Was the child so young that Cicero had not yet heard of his birth? Was their relationship more intellectual—based on debating points of literature, history, and philosophy—than personal? Or were Cicero and Nepos rarely in touch by this late point in Cicero's life?

Other comments by Cicero are even more difficult to assess. Atticus once joked that he was inferior to Nepos just as Ajax was inferior to Achilles. Cicero corrected his friend, saying that Atticus was not second–best but, was, like Achilles, the best of all men, while Nepos should be considered an "immortal".[24] Is Cicero suggesting that Nepos' talents truly place him in another class? Or is Cicero making a now obscure joke at Nepos' expense? Likewise, what could Cicero have meant in another letter when he chides Nepos, saying "to top it off you ambushed me with false gifts!" (*hoc restituit a te fictis aggrederer donis!*).[25] Is Cicero's indignation sincere? The pretentious introduction, the derogatory *fictis*, the unusual imperfect passive of *aggrederer*, and the surprising conclusion—what are "false gifts"?—suggest a semi–serious or even jocular tone, as Cicero feigns annoyance with a close friend. But without context, we cannot be sure.

Despite the apparent coolness of their relationship, Nepos had enormous respect for Cicero's political talents. He composed a lengthy (but sadly lost) biography for his friend. Reflecting on Cicero's letters, Nepos effused that the statesman had "not only predicted the events that did take place during his life, but had even prophesized those events that are now coming to pass".[26] Nepos also greatly esteemed Cicero's eloquence and praised his potential as a historian, going so far as to declare that Cicero's murder had not only deprived Rome of a great statesman, but

---

philosophers: Lactantius, *Divine Institutes* 3.15.10 and Augustine, *Unfinished Work Against Julian* 4.43.
23 Cicero, *Letters to Atticus* 16.14.4.
24 *Ibid.*, 16.5.5.
25 Priscan, *Institutes* 8.4.17.
26 Nepos, *Life of Atticus* 16.4.

denied to Latin historiography the same polish and elegance that Cicero's labors had furnished to oratory and philosophy. Cicero, in turn, respected Nepos' aesthetic judgment and his knowledge of oratory and historical writing. After Cicero was assassinated, Nepos helped Atticus publish the statesman's letters. Nepos would later say that these letters captured the truth of events better than any history.[27]

Catullus

Nepos must have already earned a reputation as a learned historian by the 50s BC, when Catullus, the young poet and a fellow emigrant from northern Italy, dedicated a collection of his poems to the scholar (Catullus 1):

cui dono lepidum novum libellum	"To whom do I give this modern, elegant booklet
arida modo pumice expolitum?	Just now polished with a dry pumice stone?
Corneli, tibi: namque tu solebas	To you, Cornelius. For you were accustomed
meas esse aliquid putare nugas.	To think my trifles worthwhile.
Iam tum, cum ausus es unus Italorum	Even then, when you alone of all Italians dared
omne aevum tribus explicare cartis...	To unfold all of history in three scrolls...
Doctis, Iuppiter, et laboriosis!	Scholarly, by Jupiter, and full of effort!
Quare habe tibi quidquid hoc libelli—	Therefore take this booklet, whatever it is,
qualecumque, quod, o patrona virgo,	And whatever it is worth, and, patron maiden,
plus uno maneat perenne saeclo!	Let it endure for more than one cycle.

Reading the poem, we learn that Nepos valued Catullus' poetry in the past and that Catullus believes that Nepos will appreciate his latest effort. Catullus suggests that his poetry shares some affinities with Nepos' (lost) *Chronica*, a concise universal history. Several phrases in Catullus' dedicatory poem indicate that the poet was familiar with Nepos' writings. Nepos was fond of characterizing the excellence of his subjects by noting that they were the only man (*unus*) to have accomplished some notable achievement. He also twice describes the process of the writing of history by using the verb *explicare*. These favorite terms influenced Catullus' own praise of Nepos as the man who "alone of all Italians" (*unus Italorum*) had "dared to explain"

---

27 Fronto, *Letter to Marcus* 1.7; Nepos, *Life of Atticus* 16.3–4.

Roman and Greek history (*ausus es...explicare*). The description of Nepos' work as "scholarly" (*doctis*) engages a key interpretive term for Catullus, indicating a laudable talent for composing and appreciating works that flaunt specialized (or even arcane) knowledge of history, language and myth. Through these verbal echoes of Nepos' work—and since so many of Nepos' texts are now lost, there may well be more that are now obscure to us—Catullus further associates his poetry with his friend's historical works.

Yet Catullus' praise of Nepos is not without ambiguity: is Nepos' history "full of effort" (*laboriosis*) because it is the laudable product of intense scholarship or because it is a chore to read—or perhaps both? For Catullus, *labor* need not suggest a lack of craftsmanship or pleasure. He describes his playful day spent composing poems with his friend Licinius as a *labor*.[28] And he calls the *Zmyrna*—a dense, learned poem over which his friend Cinna labored for nine years—a "little monument" and a "personal favorite".[29]

Whatever teasing ambiguity may animate the poem, Catullus' decision to dedicate his collection to Nepos confirms the esteem that the poet had for the scholar. It also suggests that Nepos enjoyed a lofty reputation among Catullus' Roman audience, since we would expect Catullus to dedicate his collection to a figure who would bring credit to his poetry. Their personal connection may have been strengthened by a mutual distaste for Mammura, Caesar's sybaritic associate, whom Catullus reviled in several poems. Nepos also criticized Mamurra, observing that he was the first Roman to cover his walls with marble, an innovation that exhibited his "utter lack of class".[30] Many years later, Nepos would return the compliment of Catullus' dedication by praising his deceased friend as one of the finest poets of his lifetime, ranking him as the equal of the magnificent didactic poet Lucretius.[31]

---

[28] Catullus 50.
[29] *Ibid.*, 95.
[30] Pliny, *Natural History* 36.48.
[31] Nepos, *Life of Atticus* 12.

2. Reading Nepos

When reading Nepos' *Lives*, one is immediately struck by their straightforward style. Nepos' syntax is, for the most part, clear and uncomplicated. His more complex sentences unfold in regular patterns, and he pays studious attention to signaling the circumstances in which action takes place and the connection of one thought to the next. He shows a fondness for antithesis, alliteration (e.g. *quotiēnscumque cum eō congressus est*, 1.2), and the occasional wordplay or pun. His vocabulary is similar to that found in Cicero and his contemporaries, but is more limited in scope, allowing even novice readers to spare the dictionary.

The Romans too deemed Nepos suitable for novices, even if Nepos himself did not set out to create a schoolbook. For modern readers, his simple, regular style provides a useful counterpoint to the more artful and varied grammar, vocabulary, and techniques found in more illustrious authors. Like many other Roman academics, encyclopedists, and chroniclers—e.g. Velleius Paterculus, Valerius Maximus, and Suetonius—Nepos wrote in what has been called a "middle style", a blend of simple and ornate sentences that mixes colloquialisms and archaisms. Having read Nepos, what makes Cicero Ciceronian, Caesar Caesarian, or Tacitus Tacitean will be all the more recognizable. Nepos may suffer in comparison to these masters of Latin prose style, who deploy with more elegance and creativity the linguistic and stylistic capacities that make Latin such a subtle and powerful medium for communication. But then, there are precious few writers of any era or in any language that could withstand such comparison. As we shall see, the motivation for his simple style and the decisions he made about what to include in his *Lives* can be explained by two additional factors: the aims and process of biographical writing in antiquity and the audience for whom Nepos wrote.

© Bret Mulligan, CC BY 4.0 http://dx.doi.org/10.11647/OBP.0068.02

Four Favorite Constructions

1. Connective Relatives and Demonstratives: Nepos is very careful to signal how a new sentence relates to the preceding thought. His favorite means of doing so is the connective relative, which appears at the start of over a dozen sentences in the *Life* (*AG* §308f). For example: *Ad* **quem** *cum lēgātī vēnissent* (2.2); **Quem** *etsī multa stultē cōnārī vidēbat* (8.3). Nepos will also use a demonstrative (*hic, ille, is*) to the same purpose. Often a connective will displace a word or phrase that would otherwise come at the start of a sentence, as when the subordinating conjunction *cum* is superseded by *ad quem* (2.2).

2. Ablative Absolutes: The ablative absolute is a construction favored by most Roman authors, especially those who are recounting events. Nepos is no exception, and ablative absolutes are common in the condensed narrative that dominates the second half of the *Life*. Nepos will even include two ablative absolutes in a single sentence (e.g. 5.1, 9.3, 10.1). Because of Nepos' preference for clear connections between sentences, ablative absolutes will often follow a connective: *Illī, dēspērātīs rēbus...* (8.2); *Hās, praesentibus prīncipibus...*(9.3); *ille, īnscientibus iīs...*(9.4); or a noun indicating a change in subject: *Poenus, illūsīs Crētēnsibus omnibus...* (10.1); *Tabellārius, ducis nāve dēclārātā suīs...*(11.2); *Eumenēs, solūtā epistulā...* (11.3).

3. Featured Prepositions and Conjunctions: Nepos' condensed style features an abundance of prepositions. For example, the preposition *in* is the third most common word in the *Life*. Nepos shows an unusual affinity for *apud* (15 times) and *adversus* (6 times), prepositions used more sparingly by most authors. Conversely, Nepos avoids some common prepositions, such as *inter* and *per*, each of which appears only once in the *Life*. Throughout his works, Nepos displays an affinity for the conjunctions *nam*, which signals that a sentence will justify or explain the preceding statement (AG §324h), and *enim*, used to introduce an example that explains a generalization found in the previous sentence.

4. Syncopation of Perfects: Nepos routinely shortens verbs in all tenses of the perfect system. For example, we find *superārit* for *superāverit* (1.1, see also 7.4, 7.7, 11.5), *comperisset* for *comperivisset* (2.2, see also 2.3, 6.1, 12.5), and *cēlāris* for *cēlāveris* (2.6).

Three Key Words

1. *Amīcitia*: refers to the asymmetrical relationships between patrons and clients rather than to "friendship" in the modern sense (2.4; *amīcus*: 2.6, 10.2; *inimīcissimus*: 7.3, 12.2).

2. *Callidus*: "extreme cleverness", a term Nepos uses to characterize the audacious Hannibal (9.2) and the cautious Fabius Maximus (5.2), whose strategic foresight allowed the Romans to recover from the military catastrophes they suffered at Hannibal's hands.

3. *Prūdentia*: Hannibal's cardinal virtue, according to Nepos—the ability to perceive a situation in its entirety and act accordingly (1.1, 11.7; *imprūdente* in 2.6).

Why Write Biography?

What motivated Nepos to write biographies? Unlike historians, who sought to commemorate the great achievements of previous generations and to provide examples of past successes and failures to help generals and statesmen navigate analogous situations in the present, ancient biographers focused on providing a moral education for their readers. By reading about the amazing exploits and remarkable virtues of great men, Roman readers would be inspired to conduct themselves with honor and to strive towards similar greatness. Character would be trained through the study of character. Biography, therefore, had an intrinsic value for all readers, no matter how humble, as they could observe examples of noble or iniquitous action and model their behavior accordingly, even if the circumstances of their lives were more limited than those experienced by the most preeminent figures in a given profession. As Nepos observes in his *Life of Timotheus*, the greatness of a military triumph is self-evident, but such achievements cannot be fully appreciated unless their causes are explored.[1] Nepos, however, did not seek causes in the grand patterns of history or culture as a historian might. Instead Nepos believed that "a man's character fashions his fate" (*sui cuique mores fingunt fortunam hominibus*).[2]

---

1   Nepos, *Life of Timotheus* 4.5–6.
2   Nepos, *Life of Atticus* 11.6.

It was for the same reason that the Greek biographer Plutarch (ca. 40–120 CE), Nepos' successor in composing parallel lives of Greek and Roman statesmen, justifies his decision to write biography rather than history:

> ...it is not always prominent actions that reveal virtue or vice but often an insignificant affair or a turn of phrase or a joke that reveals more about someone's character than the sieges of cities, grand tactics, and battles in which thousands of men fall.[3]

It is this, the "full picture of a man's character and life" (*imaginem consuetudinis atque vitae*), that has the potential to transform impressive achievements into educational examples.[4] Of course biography also offers the inherent pleasure of reading about the great adventures and rare achievements of great men, often undertaken in exotic locations. It is no surprise that today biography remains among the most popular and best-selling genres of non-fiction.

In his concise biographies, Nepos focuses our attention on those episodes in which his subjects exhibit their exemplary qualities. The biographies of commanders, however, posed a special challenge for the biographer. Hannibal's chief virtue, in the estimation of Nepos, was his *prudentia*, or military brilliance. But lengthy descriptions of battlefield tactics, detailed accounts of troop maneuvers, and the quotation of rousing pre-battle speeches were appropriate topics for history, not biography. Indeed, Nepos expressed anxiety that biography was ever at risk of morphing into history. Speaking of the general Pelopidas, he says, "I fear that if I were to detail his exploits, I will no longer seem to be recounting his life, but writing history" (*ne non vitam eius enarrare, sed historiam videar scribere*).[5] Nepos, therefore, elaborates well-chosen anecdotes to illustrate Hannibal's virtue. Thus we read about his cunning ruse to conceal his wealth from rapacious Cretans; how he deployed tactical oxen to elude a pursuing army (they had flaming bundles of sticks affixed between their horns); and the weaponized jars of snakes he used to defeat a superior naval force, while his stunning victories at Trebia, Trasimene, and Cannae are only mentioned in passing. To do any more would violate the spirit of Nepos' project and his attempt to carve out a distinctive identity for biography in Roman literature.

---

3   Plutarch, *Life of Alexander* 2.
4   Nepos, *Life of Epamonidas* 1.3–4.
5   Nepos, *Life of Pelopidas* 1.

Nepos and Non–Roman Cultures

To seek out the best lessons of noble conduct, Nepos decided that he would not restrict his study to notable Romans; instead, he would present the noble characters of Romans and non–Romans alike. Evaluating the morality and virtue of non–Romans, however, presented a challenge for Nepos and his contemporary Roman readers. As he observes in the *Preface* to his biographies of foreign commanders, customs differ between nations, since they arise from different "national traditions" (*maiorum instituta*). Consequently, Nepos warns that his readers should not be shocked to see illustrious foreigners engaging in behavior that would seem scandalous or reprehensible if undertaken by a Roman. Yet, despite Nepos' protestations, the cultural differences raised by Nepos are inevitably trivial. A Greek might dance or play the flute or marry his half–sister, but all good men—Greek, Roman, or even Carthaginian—display intelligence, courage, and loyalty, and so reveal themselves as suitable models for the behavior of even the most upright Roman reader. Ultimately, cultural difference is an illusion since, according to Nepos, "the nature of all states is the same" (*eandem omnium civitatum esse naturam*).[6]

The Biographical Tradition in Greece and Rome

Nepos may well have been the first author to produce a collection of biographies on different professionals. This innovative project, however, drew on a rich tradition of Greek and Roman authors who had praised famous men—and the rare woman. Today, biography is generally expected to provide a full and detailed account of a person's life, from birth to death (or at least up to the present). In antiquity, the genre of biography was slow to coalesce and encompassed a range of approaches, styles, and traditions, many of which left traces on Nepos' varied collection. Of course, the deeds of a person's life, his upbringing, and motivations are intrinsic components of any historical account that moves beyond a simple recitation of events to describe people in action. Nevertheless, it is biography's focus on the experiences of a single, extraordinary individual rather than a collective or cooperative event that differentiates biography from other forms of historical writing.

---

6   Nepos, *Life of Miltiades* 6.

The origins of biography as a distinct genre can be found in Classical Greece. Biographical elements feature prominently in the writings of Plato and Xenophon, in particular those that deal with the trial and death of their mentor, Socrates. Several of Xenophon's other works reveal a keen interest in commemorating the exemplary characters of extraordinary individuals. In his biographical novel, *The Education of Cyrus*, Xenophon creates an idealized portrait of a Persian king by documenting Cyrus' ancestry, upbringing, and the events of his youth. Xenophon also composed a biographical eulogy for his friend, the Spartan king Agesilaus, in which he recounts Agesilaus' life in chronological order before concluding with an extensive catalogue of the king's manifold virtues.

Aristotle never wrote biography, but his work on ethics—or those principles that guide a person's behavior—inspired a host of authors to explore the qualities that are distinctive to an individual's character. Some of these authors catalogued the types of characters that appeared in literature; others sought insights about the characters of great philosophers and poets. During the period of scholarly experimentation in the fourth and third centuries BC, many Greek authors composed works that were essentially biographical in nature, often with the aim of exposing the truth about a figure's character. Only fragments of works by these Hellenistic authors survive—e.g. Sotion, who wrote thirteen books on the succession of teachers and their pupils in the various philosophical schools. In what remains, however, we can discern the essential features that would come to define the genre of biography: utilization of multiple sources in determining the truth about a person's character, which was revealed by assessing their behavior and lifestyle often through the evidence of minor anecdotes rather than the great achievements that would be the focus of a proper historical account.

The Hellenistic period also witnessed a sustained interest in three quite different men: Alexander the Great, Homer, and Aesop, the writer of fables. While scholars focused their attention on the lives of generals, philosophers, and poets, many anecdotes about the members of this larger–than–life trio evolved through a symbiotic relationship between folk tradition and scholarship, in which a democratic, oral, or sub–literary tradition of storytelling provided material that scholars would elaborate and correct. Meanwhile, biographical writing about "great men", which had long been a subordinate component of the writing of history, began to take on a more central role in the historiographical projects of many authors. The fourth–century historian Theopompus was praised for examining "even the hidden reasons for actions and the motives of their agents, and the feelings in their hearts".[7] The historian Polybius, who composed a lost work on the general and statesman Philopoemen, would even claim that elucidating the upbringing and character of important figures was more vital to his goals as a historian than traditional subjects, such as the founding of cities.[8]

If Greek literature provided a variety of models for describing the lives of famous men, Roman aristocratic families had long fostered the commemoration of their worthy ancestors. Of particular importance for the development of Roman biography were the *laudationes funebres*, the "graveside eulogies" that extolled the achievements of the deceased and the glories of his prestigious ancestors. Rome's relentless climate of political competition also promoted a vibrant tradition of autobiographical writing by ambitious Romans, who sought to spread word of their successes — and excuse their failures. Among the over six hundred works composed by Varro (116–27 BC) were two autobiographies and a biographical work on poets. Nepos may have been inspired to juxtapose illustrious Greeks and Romans in different professions by Varro's *Imagines*, a compilation of seven hundred portraits of philosophers, poets, kings, dancers, and other famous men. Each portrait seems to have been accompanied by a short epigram and commentary in prose. Nepos' biographies doubtlessly owe a great deal to these earlier efforts by Greek and Roman authors. The existence of models and influences, however, should not diminish the achievement of the *Lives*, which refashioned Greek and Roman history and culture through the lens of biography, while elevating Roman achievements to the same level of prestige enjoyed by the luminaries of Greece.

Nepos' Audience

Nepos' simple style can be attributed to the audience for whom he wrote. He claims that he was not writing for other historians, but instead for the "general public" (*vulgus*).[9] Because such readers did not know Greek, they had little or no access to the history of the world that Rome had conquered or to biographies about the non–Romans who had shaped it. Nepos admits that some critics will find his biographies "trivial" (*leve*) and "unworthy"

---

7   Theopompus, 6 (Usher trans.).
8   Polybius, 10.21.4.
9   Nepos, *Life of Pelopidas* 1.

(*non satis dignum*) of the great men that they seek to immortalize.[10] But Nepos' simple style would permit any literate Roman to learn about the characters of these great men. His project, therefore, sought to harness historical figures for the moral education of a non–elite audience. Lest we underestimate his original audience, we should note that Nepos is rarely heavy–handed when holding up one of his subjects to praise or blame. Avoiding explicit moralizing comments, Nepos instead deploys anecdotes to suggest proper behavior. Since his work targeted non–elite readers through simple, concise language, it should come as no surprise that editors in late antiquity found his biographies worthy of reproduction and dissemination. And so six centuries after their composition, Nepos still found an eager new audience for his biographies, one that would ensure that at least some of his writings would survive to be read in turn by you, over two millennia after Nepos first conceived of his project.

---

10   Nepos, *Preface* 1.

3. Historical Context and Hannibal

Early History of Carthage

Legend holds that Carthage was founded around 825 BC by Dido. Dido had fled from the city of Tyre to escape her murderous brother Pygmalion. Archaeological evidence confirms that Phoenician traders from Tyre founded the city of Qart–Ḥadašt—or "New City", as Carthage was known in its native language—in the second half of the ninth century BC. The settlement of Carthage was part of a centuries–long pattern of colonization by the Phoenicians in the eastern Mediterranean aimed at dominating the lucrative trade in tin, gold, silver, and copper. Eventually the Phoenicians established over 300 coastal colonies throughout North Africa and the Iberian Peninsula (Hispania).

By the third century BC, an independent Carthage had grown into one of the more powerful states in the Mediterranean, controlling much of the coast of western North Africa, Sardinia, and Corsica, along with sections of Sicily and the Iberian Peninsula. The city itself grew to be the second largest in the ancient Mediterranean, behind only Alexandria, the magnificent capital of Ptolemaic Egypt. With its powerful fleet, Carthage dominated trade throughout the western Mediterranean and even into the Atlantic.

As the city grew in size and power during the seventh century BC, it progressively asserted its independence from Tyre, founding colonies of its own and expanding its territory in Africa. Even so, Carthage continued to signal its allegiance to its mother city by dispatching an annual embassy to Tyre's temple of Melquart, the city's patron deity.

© Bret Mulligan, CC BY 4.0   http://dx.doi.org/10.11647/OBP.0068.03

22   Cornelius Nepos, *Life of Hannibal*

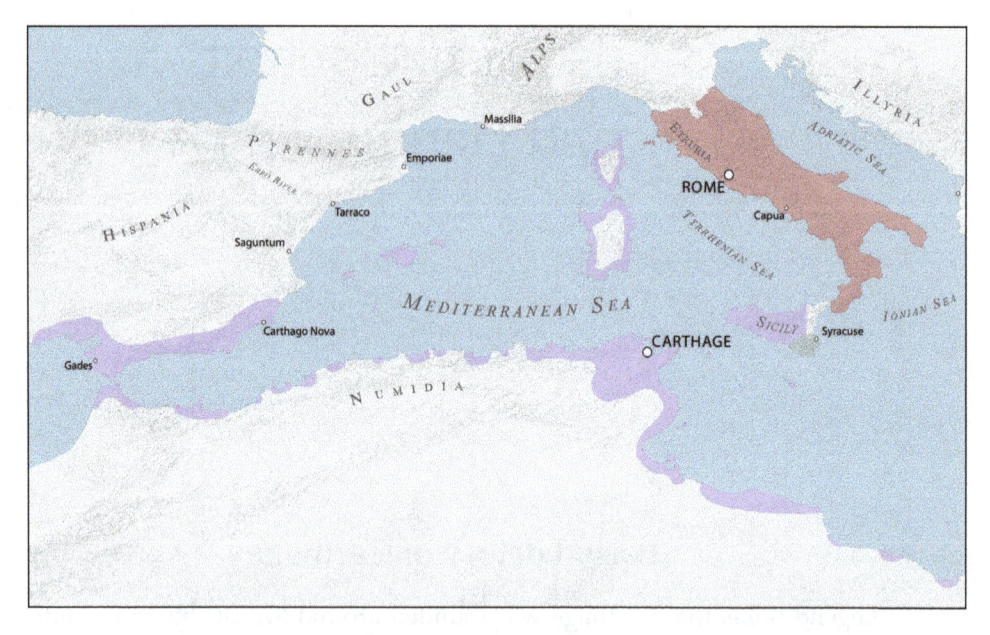

2. Carthaginian and Roman territory on the eve of the First Punic War.[1]

3. *Dido Building, Carthage* (1815) by J. M. W. Turner.[2]

---

1   Adapted with permission from images © Ancient World Mapping Center, CC BY-NC-ND. http://awmc.unc.edu/wordpress/alacarte/
2   Now at the National Gallery, London. Wikimedia, https://commons.wikimedia.org/wiki/File:Turner_-_Dido.jpg

After Tyre was conquered by the Babylonians in the early sixth century, the Phoenician colonies in the western Mediterranean turned to powerful Carthage for protection and support against their Greek rivals. Old Phoenician colonies, such as Utica and Gades in Hispania, became bound by treaty to Carthage. While Roman allies participated in a mutual defensive organization under the leadership of Rome, which gradually integrated its allies by granting their people rights and even citizenship, Carthage preferred to extract punitive taxes from its looser confederation of subjects and subject allies. These taxes were used in turn to finance Carthage's fleet and to pay mercenary soldiers. Carthage had slowly evolved from a colony to the capital of a new empire.

Despite their extensive contact with their Greek neighbors and Libyan subjects, the Carthaginians retained their Punic language, a dialect of Phoenician and a Semitic language related to Hebrew. Punic would long outlast Carthage's empire. It was still spoken in northern Africa as late as the fifth century AD, but died out soon thereafter, leaving only a few inscriptions and scattered quotations as witnesses. The Carthaginians also retained distinctive customs, including the sacrifice of infants to Baal Hammon and his consort Tanit, a practice that had long since been abandoned in Tyre and the other Semitic kingdoms of the Levant. Recently, scholars have questioned whether the Carthaginians engaged in widespread child sacrifice, or if it was reserved for especially dire moments, or if the substantial archaeological evidence indicating such sacrifice has been misinterpreted, colored by the biased accounts of Carthage's enemies, from whom we derive most of our information about the city and its people. It remains a controversial question.

As the head of a Punic coalition, Carthage forged an anti–Greek alliance with the Etruscans, who controlled Rome until the late sixth century BC. They also courted the support of the far–off Persians, who were attempting to conquer the Greeks in the eastern Mediterranean. It was said in antiquity that on the same day (in 480 BC) the united eastern Greeks destroyed the fleet of the Persian King Xerxes at Salamis, a coalition of western Greeks routed a Carthaginian force at Himera in Sicily. This coincidence is almost certainly a later fabrication, but it does demonstrate that events throughout the eastern and western Mediterranean were understood to be part of one grand narrative in antiquity. After their defeat at Himera, the Carthaginians avoided open conflict with the Greeks in Sicily, turning their attention instead to expanding their territory in Africa, exploring and colonizing the Atlantic coast (perhaps as far south as modern Cameroon), and developing their inland trade routes to the south.

As Carthage grew into a major military power, its political system was evolving from a monarchy to a more inclusive republican form of government—a transformation experienced by many other city-states throughout the ancient Mediterranean at this time, including Rome. Eventually, Carthage's government came to be led by two annually elected magistrates (*suffetes* or "kings"); a Council of Elders (the *adirim* or "Mighty Ones") consisting of the leading men of the city; and an assembly of citizens who could arbitrate between the suffetes and Council when they were at odds. Unlike the Romans, whose annually-elected magistrates managed both civilian and military affairs, the Carthaginians created a separate office of general, who was appointed for a specific mission. Because these generals often continued in office until that mission was completed, they could accumulate considerable influence. Their power was checked, however, by the Council of 104 judges, who had the authority to convict and crucify delinquent generals. Carthage's political system was often praised in antiquity: Aristotle thought Carthage possessed one of the best constitutions. In practice, however, a single preeminent family often acquired political supremacy for extended periods of time. Sometimes this family would rule collaboratively with other members of the aristocracy; at others, it would exercise near absolute authority in the city.

To understand the savage tenacity displayed by the Carthaginians and Romans in the Second Punic War, it is necessary to understand the previous conflicts between the two powers. Early in their history, Rome and Carthage signed several treaties of friendship and even fought as (somewhat unenthusiastic) allies against adventuring Greek potentates. But Rome's growing involvement with Carthage's Greek adversaries in southern Italy and Sicily—combined with Rome's traditional fear of powerful neighbors—caused increasing tensions between the two powers. Beginning in 264 BC, Rome and Carthage would fight three brutal wars for control of the western Mediterranean. Collectively these conflicts are known as the Punic Wars after the Latin word for "Phoenician", *Poenus*.

First Punic War (264–241 BC)

The seeds of the First Punic War had been sown in the 280s BC when a small band of unemployed Italian mercenaries, known as the *Mamertines* or the "Sons of Mars", occupied the strategic town of Messana in northwest Sicily. Situated on the narrow straight that separates Italy from Sicily,

Messana controlled commerce and communications between Sicily and the mainland. When Hiero II of Syracuse attempted to dislodge the Mamertines in 265, they enlisted the aid of a nearby Carthaginian fleet, whose swift intervention forced Hiero to withdraw. The Mamertines soon regretted the Carthaginian occupation and appealed to Rome for protection, citing their status as Italians. Rome was hesitant to become entangled in a conflict outside of Italy or to come to the aid of the piratical Mamertines. Indeed, Rome had only a few years before executed a similar group who had occupied the Italian town of Rhegium. Yet Rome's fear of a Carthaginian stronghold so close to Italy—and greed for plunder in what they assumed would be a short war against Syracuse—outweighed their concerns. The Romans, under the command of the consul Appius Claudius Caudex, invaded Sicily and marched to the Mamertines' aid.

When the Mamertines learned that the Romans were approaching, they persuaded the Carthaginian general to withdraw his forces from the city. The general, regretting this decision to abandon the city, took the fateful steps of allying with Hiero. The combined Carthaginian and Syracusan forces then besieged Messana. After attempts to negotiate a truce failed, Carthage and Rome began hostilities. Both sides were confident of a quick and decisive victory. Neither side anticipated the horror that was to come: a ferocious, generation-long war, which would witness many large-scale disasters and innumerable small-scale atrocities. This war would transform the Roman and Carthaginian empires, upend the balance of power in the western Mediterranean, and set the stage for Hannibal's avenging assault on Italy.

It was in Sicily that the war began, and in and around Sicily where most of the fighting took place. Roman forces swiftly crossed over into Sicily, captured Messana, and then forced Syracuse to capitulate. Carthage, after crucifying the tentative general who had lost the strategic initiative by permitting Rome's invasion, adopted the cautious strategy that they had honed in generations of intermittent fighting against the Sicilian Greeks. Their mercenary army, operating from fortified towns, would harass the allies of Rome and Syracuse, eventually sapping their will to continue the fight, while allowing Carthage to make opportunistic gains whenever an opportunity arose. It was a defensive strategy, designed to preserve a status quo that was quite satisfactory to the Carthaginians. But the Carthaginians would soon realize that the Romans were a decidedly more powerful and more lethal foe than the loose confederations of Greek city-states that they had previously fought.

In 262, the Romans moved against the fortified city of Agrigentum. After Roman forces defeated a Carthaginian army that had been sent to lift the siege, they brutally sacked the city. Rome was not interested in restoring the status quo; they sought to expel Carthage from Sicily. The sack of Agrigentum stiffened Carthaginian resolve. Attempts by Rome to follow up on their success by capturing other Carthaginian cities in Sicily proved costly and ineffective. A bloody strategic stalemate developed in which cities would be taken and switch sides only to be retaken or betrayed again.

Rome realized that defeating Carthage would require a navy that could attack the Carthaginian homeland in Africa and thwart Carthage's ability to resupply its beleaguered coastal cities in Sicily. To counter Carthage's naval superiority, Rome undertook a rapid armament program, building and training a navy in a matter of months. After early losses at sea, Romans determined that they could exploit their own superiority in close-quarter fighting by equipping their ships with a hooked gangplank—the *corvus* or "crow"—that allowed Roman marines to grapple, board, and capture Carthaginian ships. Eventually, in 256 a Roman fleet of over 300 ships and 150,000 men defeated the Carthaginians off Cape Ecnomus. The path to Africa lay open.

The African campaign of 256–255 met with early success. Romans under the consul Atilius Regulus ravaged the African countryside and won a smashing victory that forced Carthage to sue for peace. But when Rome offered terms that were excessively punitive, Carthage hired the Spartan Xanthippus to reorganize its army and plan the defense of its territory. Xanthippus lured Regulus into a battle on open ground, where Carthage's war elephants and its advantage in cavalry overwhelmed the Romans. Only 2,000 Romans—from a force of over 15,000—survived to be evacuated by the Roman fleet. The consul Regulus was captured (he would later be tortured to death). Compounding the disaster, a storm wrecked nearly the entire evacuation fleet before it reached Italy. As many as 90,000 men drowned, taking with them Rome's hopes of invading Africa and forcing a quick end to the war. Attention turned again to Sicily and the brutal war of attrition.

While Rome regrouped and rebuilt its fleet, Carthage enjoyed a brief period of success in Sicily. Rome, however, soon regained the offensive, capturing numerous cities in rapid succession and securing all but the westernmost region of the island. Yet Rome failed to press its advantage.

Since they sought the capitulation of Carthage, they sent their fleet in 253 to raid the Libyan coast, where it was lost in a storm—another 150 ships lost and over 60,000 men drowned. In the meantime, Carthage was able to transport 100 war elephants to Sicily, further deterring the Romans, who were mindful of the role the elephants played in the destruction of Regulus' army. Rome would require two years before it could resume serious offensive operations, when they besieged the stronghold of Lilybaeum, the lynchpin of Carthage's remaining defenses in Sicily.

Old patterns soon reasserted themselves. The Romans were unable to prevent the Carthaginians from resupplying the garrison by sea. Indeed, the daring Carthaginian admiral Ad Herbal often simply sailed his better-trained and nimbler ships past the Roman fleet in broad daylight. Provoked by this humiliating display of superior Carthaginian seamanship, the consul Publius Claudius Pulcher prepared a surprise assault against the Carthaginian fleet at Drepana. Appearing outside the harbor at dawn and with the element of surprise, Pulcher appeared to be on the brink of a decisive victory that might well have won Rome the war. Instead, the Roman assault was fatally delayed as they awaited a favorable omen, allowing Ad Herbal to clear the harbor. Pulcher's fleet, now hopelessly outmaneuvered and trapped against the Sicilian coast, lost ninety ships. Within days, a second Roman fleet of 120 ships and 800 transports was destroyed by a storm in eastern Sicily. The Romans would never take Lilybaeum by force; seven years would pass before the Romans had the courage and financial resources to build another fleet.

The war in Sicily was again at a stalemate. With the exhausted opponents no longer able to mount large scale operations, the war devolved into a series of small-scale ambushes and atrocities. Hamilcar Barca, Hannibal's father, began waging an audacious guerilla campaign against Roman forces and allies. Finally in 243 BC the Roman Senate resolved to resume large-scale offensive operations. A new fleet, financed by onerous loans, was constructed. After the destruction of one Carthaginian fleet by storm in 241 and another at the Battle of the Aegates Islands, a faction of wealthy landowners that favored peace came to power in Carthage. The long war drew to a close.

Rome had outlasted Carthage, which had never adapted to Rome's aggressive strategy. As Rome systematically worked to expand its territory in Sicily and pressure Carthage by invading and raiding Africa, Carthage passively reacted to Rome's moves, stubbornly fighting a defensive war geared towards not losing the conflict. Although individual Carthaginian generals displayed brilliance at sea and on land (none more so than Hamilcar), Carthage never devised a strategy to defeat the more populous Rome, which routinely absorbed horrific losses and staggering defeats only to regroup and resume the attack. Hamilcar would pass these hard-won lessons to Hannibal, who would devise a bold, aggressive strategy to defeat Rome.

As part of the terms of the peace, Carthage agreed to surrender Sicily and its naval bases on the surrounding islands to the Romans, avoid conflict with Syracuse and other Roman allies, release Roman prisoners without ransom, and pay an enormous indemnity of 3,200 talents or the equivalent of nearly 100 tons of silver. Rome, which before the war had never fought outside of Italy, now controlled a wealthy overseas territory—its first of many. Nevertheless, their victory must have been bittersweet. During the long 23 years of conflict, Rome lost over 600 ships, Carthage at least 500. As many as 50,000 Roman citizens and another 350,000 allies had been killed, most suffering horrific deaths at sea. The Carthaginians too suffered terribly in the war, a losing effort that left them economically bankrupt, deprived of their possessions in Sicily, and bereft of their signature navy. Before the war, Rome and Carthage were wary rivals with a long tradition of coexistence and even cooperation; afterwards, they were bitter enemies, each steeped in a generation of blood. For the Romans, their erstwhile allies were now seen as bloodthirsty and duplicitous. Indeed, the phrase *Punica fides* ("Carthaginian loyalty") became a byword for the most vicious kind of treachery. Romans simultaneously reviled Carthaginians as cruel and cowardly: they were said to sacrifice children and eat dogs, while being in the emasculating grip of eastern-style luxury and enervated by Africa's climate. We can assume that the same *animus* roiled the Carthaginians against the Romans. The peace, like the war, would last for 23 years. But the stage had been set for an even greater conflict, one that would push first Rome and then Carthage to the brink of destruction.

Between the Wars

Carthage's humiliating defeat and the economic depression that followed precipitated a vicious rebellion by Carthage's mercenary soldiers and African allies known as the Truceless or Mercenary War (241–237 BC). Rome, which officially supported Carthage in the conflict, nevertheless took advantage of Carthage's weakness to seize Sardinia and Corsica and to extort additional reparations. Eventually, under the leadership of Hamilcar and Hannibal's brother-in-law, Hasdrubal the Fair, Carthage was able to suppress the rebellion. Because of Hamilcar's role in rescuing Carthage from this crisis, he and his family gained considerable influence among the Carthaginian people, as well as widespread support throughout the Carthaginian government.

With its territories in Sicily, Sardinia, and Corsica lost to Rome, Hamilcar sought new conquests in Hispania, a wealthy region that included the richest silver mines in the Mediterranean. By the 220s Carthage had recovered from its defeat in the First Punic War. Meanwhile Rome, content with the status quo, recognized Carthage's gains in Hispania and turned its attention to governing its new territories and completing the conquest of northern Italy. The Romans organized Sicily and then Sardinia and Corsica as their first overseas provinces. From 225 to 222 BC, Rome pacified the Gauls in northern Italy and then began campaigning in Illyria across the Adriatic Sea. Rome's eastward expansion into Illyria, however, was cut short by unforeseen events in Hispania, events that would soon involve Rome in a fight for its very survival.

Second Punic War (218–201 BC)

In 219 BC, Hannibal laid siege to Saguntum, a coastal city in northeast Hispania that enjoyed a treaty of friendship with Rome. In 226 BC Hasdrubal the Fair signed a treaty with Rome that acknowledged Carthage's control of Hispania south of the Iber River (modern Ebro). Saguntum's status, therefore, was ambiguous: was it an ally of Rome or a ward of Carthage? When the besieged Saguntines appealed to Rome, Rome pressured the Carthaginians to recognize their alliance with Saguntum. Even as the Romans attempted to negotiate a settlement to the crisis, Hannibal captured the city after an eight-month siege. When Carthage refused Roman demands for Hannibal's extradition, both sides prepared for war.

Rome and Carthage enjoyed different military advantages than they had during the last war. Hannibal now fielded the best-trained and equipped army in the ancient world; the Romans enjoyed complete naval superiority, which they could use to invade Carthaginian territory at will. Rome expected to exploit this advantage to wage a quick, offensive war that would compel Carthage to sue for peace on Rome's terms. Hannibal, however, had a plan to restore Carthage's supremacy in the western Mediterranean. First, he would neutralize Rome's advantage at sea through a daring invasion of Italy across the Alps. Hannibal correctly saw that the presence of a foreign army in Italy would compel the Romans to abandon their planned assault on Carthage. Once across the Alps, Hannibal planned to recruit soldiers from the recently conquered regions of northern and southern Italy and convince other kingdoms in the East to join forces against Rome. At the head of this combined force, Hannibal would cut at the roots of Roman military power by disrupting the intricate web of alliances that bound the cities and peoples of Italy to Rome. It is important to note that Hannibal's goal at the start of the war was not to destroy the city or exterminate the Romans, despite the claims made by later Roman authors. Hannibal assumed that a few decisive victories in Italy would compel Rome to negotiate a new peace treaty on terms favorable to Carthage. At the least, he thought he could restore Carthaginian holdings in Sicily and Sardinia and a recognition of their empire in Hispania. Roman resolve, however, would again surprise the Carthaginians.

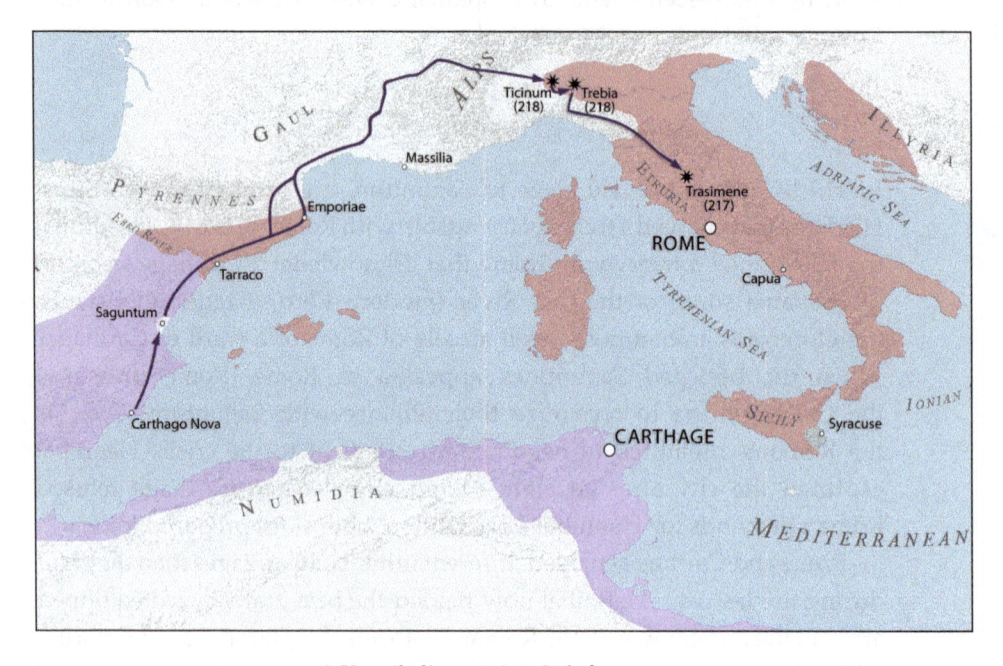

4. Hannibal's route into Italy.[3]

---

3   Adapted with permission from images © Ancient World Mapping Center, CC BY-NC-ND. http://awmc.unc.edu/wordpress/alacarte/

5. *Snow Storm. Hannibal and his Army Crossing the Alps* (1810–1812) by J. M. W. Turner.[4]

At the start of the war, the Romans assumed that Hannibal, whose army was in constant danger of being outflanked by sea, would seek to protect Carthage's hard–won territory in northern Hispania. The Roman strategy assumed that one army would pin Hannibal down in Hispania, freeing another to invade the Carthaginian homeland in Africa. But Hannibal, ever bold, seized the initiative and marched towards Italy with a large army. He evaded the first Roman army sent against him and arrived at the Alps in late 218 BC with 38,000 infantry troops, 8,000 cavalrymen, and 37 war elephants. The brutal march over the mountains in the early winter cost Hannibal nearly a third of his army and most of his irreplaceable elephants. But his gamble worked. He was able to lead an intact army into Italy. Hannibal then won a cavalry engagement at Ticinus and forced the Romans to withdraw south of the Padus River. Facing an enemy army in Italy, the Romans recalled the forces that were being marshaled for the planned invasion of Africa. Hannibal had succeeded in forestalling the invasion of Carthage. His audacity had gained him the chance to win the war in Italy.

In quick succession, Hannibal inflicted two crushing defeats on a stunned and unprepared Rome. At Trebia, 30,000 freezing Roman soldiers were lured into an ambush and killed. Hannibal then crossed the Padus River into

---

4   Now at Tate Britain, London. Wikimedia, https://commons.wikimedia.org/wiki/File:Joseph_Mallord_William_Turner_081.jpg

central Italy. Despite the shocking defeat, Rome refused to negotiate terms with the invader. In 217, the two consuls raised a new army and led it against Hannibal. At Lake Trasimene, Hannibal again demonstrated his mastery of battlefield tactics when the consul Gaius Flaminius Nepos and more than 40,000 soldiers were ambushed on the narrow path along the shore of the lake. Nearly all of the Roman soldiers in Flaminius' army were either killed or captured. After this second disaster, Rome was seized by panic and memories of the Gallic Sack of 390 BC. But still the Romans refused to surrender or even negotiate an exchange of prisoners. Instead, Fabius Maximus was elected dictator and invested with unlimited power to confront the threat to Rome.

Unlike his impetuous colleagues, Fabius accurately assessed the tactical and strategic situation facing Rome. Fabius realized that Hannibal's decisive advantage in cavalry forces made it too risky to engage him in a large-scale battle on level ground. He also recognized that Rome's superior manpower would eventually yield victory, provided that he could thwart Hannibal's strategic goal of separating Rome from her Italian allies. Fabius therefore avoided a direct confrontation with Hannibal's forces. He focused instead on protecting Rome's allies and wearing down Hannibal's army through small raids. This "Fabian" tactic of avoiding decisive battle spared Rome's soldiers and preserved Rome's alliances, but his caution lost him favor among the more aggressive-minded Roman senators who were eager to confront Hannibal, as well as many other Roman citizens whose property was being destroyed by Hannibal's army.

Unchecked, Hannibal ranged throughout Italy, eventually destroying 400 towns and capturing several large cities. In the face of such devastation, two new consuls were elected on the promise to make short work of Hannibal. Under the burning summer sky, the largest army that Rome would ever field within Italy marched to crush what they saw as Hannibal's gaggle of barbarians. Outside of the strategic town of Cannae, however, Hannibal annihilated both consular armies: as many as 70,000 Romans and allies were butchered in a single afternoon—among the worst defeats ever suffered by Rome, or indeed by any army.

Rome's allies began to waver as Hannibal's successes mounted. Several major cities revolted, as did large swaths of southern Italy. Soon after Cannae, another army was destroyed while attempting to pacify a Gallic tribe that had defected to Hannibal. Hannibal's army and his allies had killed upwards of 175,000 Roman and Italian soldiers in just over 20 months. At this moment, Philip of Macedon agreed to open a second front against Roman interests in Illyria. By almost any reckoning, Hannibal had won the war. Rome's power base had been reduced to central Italy and Sicily. It had lost the core of its army and a large portion of its military and political aristocracy, its allies were abandoning it, and rival powers were beginning to line up behind Hannibal, who must have thought he was on the verge of victory. Yet even in the face of these manifold disasters, Rome rejected even the thought of peace on Hannibal's terms. It banned public displays of mourning, refused to negotiate, and began recruiting new armies. Improbably, the war had only just begun.

In this moment of crisis, Rome resumed the Fabian strategy. Decisive battles were avoided whenever possible, allies were protected, disloyal or captured cities were slowly re–conquered. The Romans deployed their fleet to limit reinforcements from Philip of Macedonia or Carthage. They used clever diplomacy to enmesh Philip in a costly and distracting war in Greece. With the immediate crisis averted, Rome's superiority in manpower and organization eventually began to turn the tide.

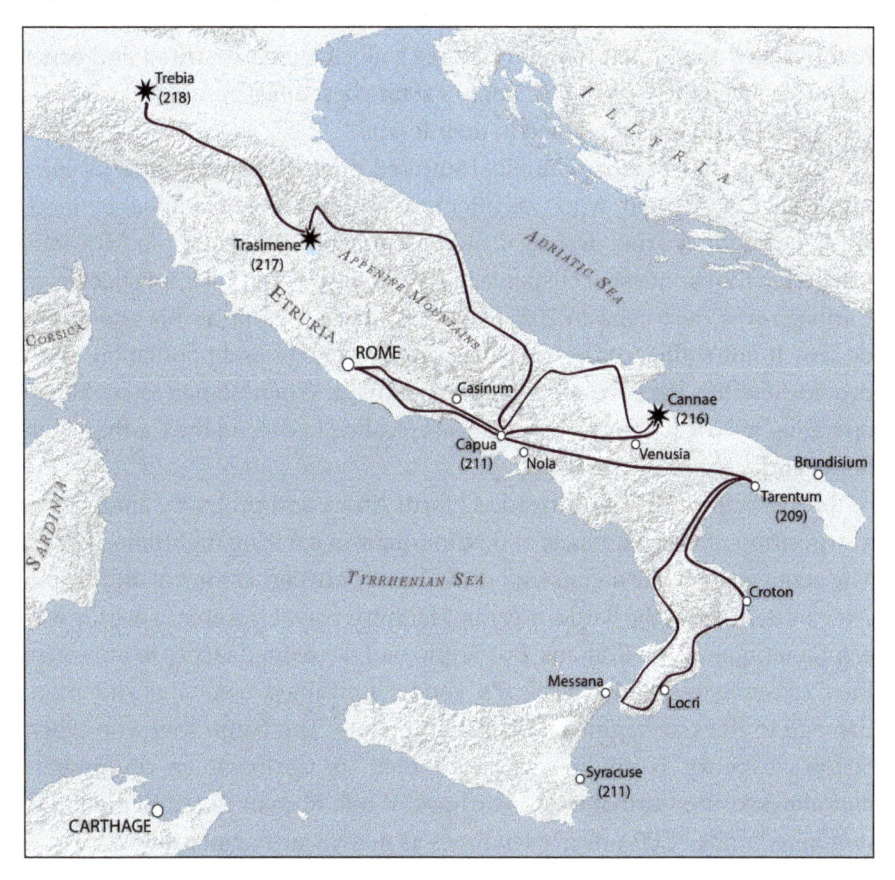

6. Hannibal's campaign in Italy.[5]

---

5   Adapted with permission from images © Ancient World Mapping Center, CC BY-NC-ND. http://awmc.unc.edu/wordpress/alacarte/

During the decade from 215 to 205 BC Rome fielded as many as seven and never fewer than four two–legion armies every year in Italy. At its peak mobilization in 212 BC, Rome fielded 25 legions and a massive fleet with over 200,000 men, which it used to conduct simultaneous operations from Hispania to Africa to the Aegean. Hannibal, who was never able to field more than three large armies at a time, was thus constantly made to react to Roman operations against his new Italian allies.

In 211, Hannibal at last marched against Rome. It would be more than 600 years before a foreign army would again marshal outside of Rome's gates. Even so, Hannibal was incapable of sustaining a prolonged siege against the well–defended city. This move was only a diversionary tactic to forestall a Roman expedition to Africa. By 209, Rome had retaken most of the cities in Italy and begun to make inroads against Carthaginian territory in Hispania. Hannibal, however, still hoped to win the war. A decade of continual war had wrecked the Italian economy. Rome's allies were exhausted and eager for peace. Even the Latin cities, Rome's staunchest allies, refused new levies, claiming that no men remained in their towns.

At this crucial juncture Hannibal suffered three disastrous setbacks. First his brother Hasdrubal, who was attempting to reinforce Hannibal by land, was killed and his army destroyed at Metaurus in 207. Then Scipio Africanus completed the conquest of Hispania in 206. Finally, a large resupply fleet from Carthage was destroyed in 205. Hannibal's daring gambit—his attempt to destroy Rome's alliances before its superior resources and population could provide it with a decisive advantage—had failed. When Roman forces began operating in North Africa, Hannibal was recalled to defend the Carthaginian homeland.

In 204, Scipio Africanus invaded North Africa and promptly annihilated a large army of Carthaginians and Numidians in a daring nighttime assault. The stage was set for a climactic showdown between Hannibal and Scipio Africanus. In 202 at the Battle of Zama, Hannibal was at last able to deploy war elephants against the Romans. But Scipio had developed tactics to minimize their effectiveness and Hannibal's young, untrained elephants did more damage to the Carthaginians than the Romans. The battle was won when Scipio's superior Numidian cavalry routed its Carthaginian counterpart and attacked the Carthaginian rear lines. While Roman losses in the battle numbered under 2,000, nearly ten times as many Carthaginians died.

Even as Hannibal attempted to regroup, Carthage sued for peace. The terms were onerous: Carthage agreed to surrender all territory outside

Africa, to wage war only with Roman permission, and to pay a massive indemnity of 5,000 talents (later raised to 10,000) over fifty years. Carthage's empire and its military power were broken. Rome stood unchallenged as the most powerful state in the western Mediterranean.

Aftermath

After the war, Carthage was beset by another financial depression, one exacerbated by the crippling burden of the indemnity owed to Rome. In the depths of this crisis, Carthage turned to Hannibal. Elected suffete, Hannibal reformed the tax system and stabilized the economy, enabling Carthage to reinvent itself from an imperial capital into a flourishing commercial hub. It is likely that Carthage constructed its famed double harbor at this time.

Carthage's revival soon provoked Roman fears of a resurgent Carthage, as well as greed for the wealth that it was so rapidly accumulating. For a time, while Rome was preoccupied with pacifying its new overseas territories in Hispania and in settling old scores with Philip of Macedon, Rome was content to profit from Carthage's prosperity. But when Carthage paid off the last of its reparations in 152, Rome ceased to benefit from Carthage's success. The Roman senator Cato the Elder began to stoke Roman eagerness for war. At the end of every speech—regardless of the subject—he was said to declare his belief that Rome must be freed from the threat of Carthage.[6] Carthage, however, scrupulously observed its obligations under the terms of the peace and even supported Rome's wars in the East. But by 150 BC relentless expansion by the Numidians, now a Roman ally, forced Carthage to act in self-defense without Roman authorization. The treaty was abrogated. Both sides prepared for war.

The following year Carthage sent ambassadors to accept peace on the terms offered by Rome. They must have expected the Romans to leverage the crisis to extort monetary and territorial concessions, as they had so many times before. After first agreeing to the demands that they surrender their weapons and deliver hundreds of children as hostages, the Romans demanded that the Carthaginians abandon their city and resettle ten miles inland, a concession that the ambassadors knew their fellow Carthaginians

---

6 Cato is often said to have concluded every speech with the same dire advice—*censeo Carthaginem esse delendam* ("I recommend that Carthage must be destroyed"), from which arose the dictum "*Carthago delenda est*" ("Carthage must be destroyed"). But it is more likely that this expression was fabricated by later authors, who sought to dramatize Cato's relentless drive to destroy the city with a single pithy phrase (Little 1934).

would never accept. Rome had at last bowed to Cato's advice: Carthage would be destroyed.

7. *The Capture of Carthage* (1539). Engraving by George Pencz.[7]

Despite their hopeless situation, the Carthaginians valiantly resisted for three years. But finally, in 146, Carthage's massive fortifications were breached by Roman forces under the command of Scipio Aemilianus, the adopted grandson of Scipio Africanus. As Carthage burned, for six days savage fighting raged from house to house. At last, 50,000 exhausted Carthaginians surrendered the citadel. So horrible was the carnage in that once magnificent city that Scipio, a man hardened by years of bloody campaigning in Hispania, was said to have wept at the sight. The surviving Carthaginians were sold into slavery. The city was abandoned and its land cursed.

It is a modern fable that Romans salted the earth to prevent anything from growing at the site. Rome, having destroyed its greatest rival, organized Carthage's African territory as a new province. The Punic language and elements of Punic culture would survive. And in time, a new settlement would grow in the ashes of the old. But this was a Roman city on the shores of a Mediterranean dominated by Rome.

---

7   Now at the Los Angeles County Museum of Art. Wikimedia, https://commons.wikimedia.org/wiki/File:Georg_Pencz_-_The_Capture_of_Carthage.jpg

Hannibal

Hannibal was born into a prestigious Carthaginian family in 247 BC, as the First Punic War (264–241 BC) was drawing to a close. In the waning years of that war, Hannibal's father, Hamilcar, had waged a brilliant guerilla campaign in Sicily and conducted daring raids against the Italian coast, earning the nickname "Barca" or "Thunderbolt", a name that was adopted by his descendants. After Carthage's calamitous defeat in that war, Hamilcar helped suppress a dangerous rebellion by Carthage's mercenaries and subject allies in North Africa (240–238 BC). After Hamilcar had rescued the Carthaginian state, he forged a new empire for Carthage in Hispania (modern Spain). It was during Hamilcar's campaigns in Hispania that Hannibal would learn the military skills that he would turn against Rome.

About Hannibal's mother, nothing is known. It is possible that she was a foreigner, since Carthaginian noblemen routinely practiced exogamy, or marriage to foreigners. Hannibal's sisters, for example, were married to royalty in Numidia, a region that comprised a substantial portion of Carthage's empire in North Africa. Hannibal had two younger brothers: Hasdrubal and Mago, both of whom served as Hannibal's lieutenants in the Second Punic War. Hamilcar famously declared that his sons were a "brood of lion cubs raised for Rome's destruction"—or so later Romans imagined.[8] About Hannibal's childhood we hear only the story of his oath of hatred against Rome, which was recounted by most ancient authors who discuss Hannibal's life in any detail, including Nepos (2.3–4). Shortly before he marched against Italy, he married an Iberian woman. If he had a son, he died young. About Hannibal's physical appearance we are ignorant, apart from a few idealized portraits on contemporary coins.

A clearer picture of Hannibal's character emerges from the many ancient historians who recounted his exploits. The Greek historian Polybius claims that Hannibal had a violent temper.[9] An anecdote from the aftermath of his defeat in the Second Punic War suggests that age and experience did little to soften his irritability. When an arrogant politician spoke against the peace treaty, an enraged Hannibal physically assaulted the speaker, dragging him from the podium.[10] Hannibal later returned to the senate and apologized for his conduct, citing his unfamiliarity with the customs of politics after a lifetime spent in military service.

---

8   Valerius Maximus, 9.3 ext.2.
9   Polybius, 3.15.9.
10 Livy, 30.37.

8. Roman bust of Hannibal. Statue in marble. Capua, Italy.[11]

The Roman historian Livy reports that he combined "the most reckless daring for undertaking risk" (*plurimum audaciae ad pericula capessenda*) with "the most judicious calm when in danger" (*plurimum consilii inter ipsa pericula*) and was "more wonderful when facing adversity than in enjoying his success".[12]

Many ancient authors observe that Hannibal could withstand extreme physical hardships and was moderate in his consumption of food and drink. The harsh realities of his life, which was spent almost entirely at war or in exile, suggest the truth of this assessment. Nevertheless, we should remember that ancient authors tend to characterize individuals as falling into one of two camps: those who were toughened by physical hardship and deprivation and those who were weakened by soft living and indulgence in luxury. These historians, therefore, perhaps tell us more about how Hannibal was thought to behave than about the man he actually was.

Most Roman sources, on which we are largely dependent, dwell on Hannibal's savagery and wickedness. According to Livy, he possessed an "inhuman cruelty, treachery worse than usual for a Carthaginian, disregard for truth and the sacred, a lack of fear towards the gods and respect for oaths and any religion".[13] Seneca the Younger offers the grim

---

11   Now at the Museo Archeologico Nazionale, Naples. Wikimedia, https://commons.wikimedia.org/wiki/File:Mommsen_p265.jpg
12   Livy, 21.4.5, 28.12.3.
13   Livy, 21.4.

vision of a depraved Hannibal gazing at a trench filled with blood and declaring "what a beautiful sight!" (*o formosum spectaculum*).[14] Like most of the testimonials preserved by hostile Roman witnesses, such anecdotes should be viewed with skepticism. At the same time, we must remember that Hannibal did engage in a vicious war in Italy for over a decade. The accounts of the atrocities that he committed while attempting to break the will of the Romans and their allies cannot be dismissed simply as the product of Roman bias. There was doubtless good reason why "Hannibal at the gates" (*Hannibal ad portas*) became shorthand for a looming crisis and an admonition used to frighten Roman children into behaving. It should be noted that Nepos omits any mention of such lurid tales, crafting, all in all, the most favorable portrait of Hannibal offered by any ancient author.

The exploits of Hannibal's life reveal a man of remarkable competence and rare abilities. He inspired breathtaking loyalty and extraordinary obedience among his troops, which included Carthaginians as well as mercenaries recruited from throughout the ancient Mediterranean. Sources recount how he slept on a military cloak, eating the food of the common soldiers and sharing their hardships. As a tactician, his genius was of the first rank. Military leaders to this day study Hannibal's victories at the battles of Trebia, Trasimene, and above all Cannae. In peacetime, he proved himself a dynamic and principled, if not always tactful, politician. Imagine the fortitude it must have taken to return to Carthage after losing a war undertaken at his initiative. Carthaginians, it should be remembered, were in the habit of crucifying defeated generals.

Hannibal not only survived—in no small part because he retained the loyalty of the army—but within a few years he was elected to the highest office in Carthage. As Carthage strained under the terms of its humiliating treaty with Rome, Hannibal worked to prevent the entrenched aristocracy from exploiting the suffering people of the city. He proved himself so successful at reorganizing Carthaginian finances that he offered to pay off early the full total of the war reparations owed to Rome. When Rome spurned the offer, Hannibal's enemies in Carthage engineered his downfall, forcing him to flee the city. In later times, his cunning determination in resisting Roman expansion made him a symbol of the downtrodden and the underdog. It is no coincidence that Hannibal was adopted as an ancestor of the Irish, who imagined themselves in the role of Carthage against the imperial might of the British Empire.

---

14   Seneca the Younger, *On Anger* 2.5.4.

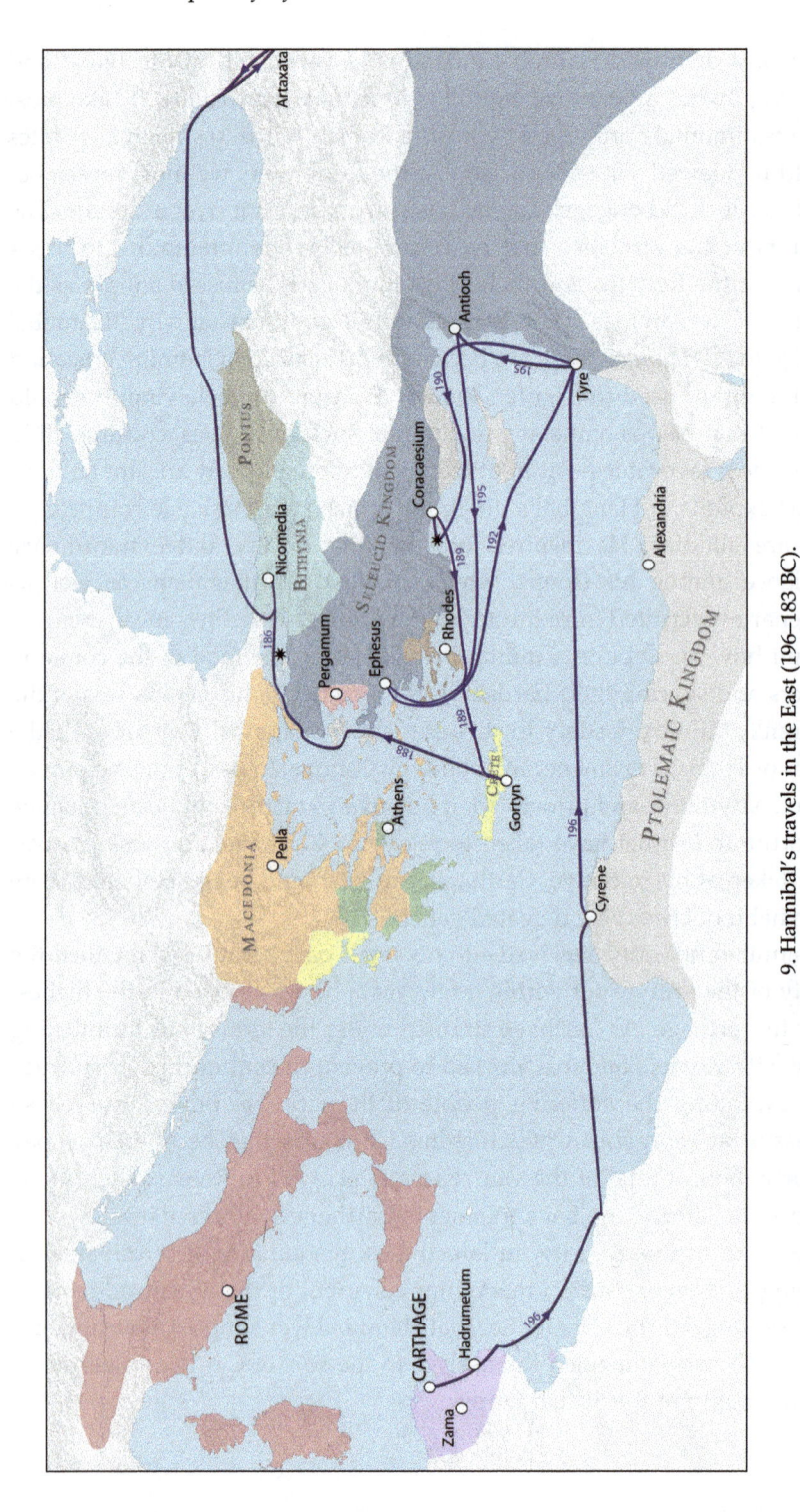

40 Cornelius Nepos, *Life of Hannibal*

9. Hannibal's travels in the East (196–183 BC). Adapted with permission from images © Ancient World Mapping Center, CC BY-NC-ND. http://awmc.unc.edu/wordpress/alacarte/

Evaluating Hannibal

The life of Hannibal grants many opportunities to wonder what might have been: what if Hannibal had reached Italy earlier in the season and thus had not lost so many troops and elephants in crossing the Alps; what if Hasdrubal had succeeded in reinforcing Hannibal from Spain; what if reinforcements had come sooner from Carthage...? And yet, one can also look at Hannibal's life as a series of fleeting tactical successes punctuating a record of strategic failures. He inherited a wealthy and expanding empire only to leave Carthage prostrate and at Rome's mercy. He failed to leverage his smashing victory at Cannae to better strategic advantage. He never devised a strategy to combat the Fabian tactics of harassment and disengagement. For all his military daring, he was unable to break Rome's hold over Italy, and misjudged the loyalty of Rome's most important allies. His diplomatic efforts failed to entice another powerful state to attack Rome in Italy. His fugitive latter days, when he fled from the court of one eastern potentate to another, bear the mark of a man obsessed with fighting a war that he had lost years before. In the memorable words of Plutarch, he was now "a tame and harmless bird that had grown too old to fly and had lost its tail feathers".[15] Indeed what seemed his only enduring success—the reinvention of Carthage as a vibrant commercial power—would eventually stoke Roman fear of renewed Carthaginian power and greed for the fruits of its enemy's newfound prosperity. In 146 BC, less than forty years after Hannibal's death, Carthage would be razed to the ground by Scipio Aemilianus, the son of Hannibal's great nemesis, Scipio Africanus. Hannibal had achieved immortality—but at a terrible cost. This melancholy tension is perhaps best captured by this short poem by Robert Frost:

> Was there even a cause too lost,
> Ever a cause that was lost too long,
> Or that showed with the lapse of time too vain
> For the generous tears of youth and song?
> — "Hannibal" (1928)

---

15 Plutarch, *Life of Flamininus* 21.

Bibliography

Recommended Works on Nepos and Ancient Biography

Hägg, T. 2012. *The Art of Biography in Antiquity*. Cambridge University Press, 187–196. Available at http://books.google.com/books?id=NhLQbSdTKooC

Pryzwansky, M. 2009–2010. "Cornelius Nepos: Key Issues and Critical Approaches". *Classical Journal* 105.2: 99–108.

Stem, R. 2012. *The Political Biographies of Cornelius Nepos*. University of Michigan Press. Available at http://books.google.com/books?id=cmX_UgTGLdQC

Titchener, F. 2002. "Cornelius Nepos and the Biographical Tradition". *Greece & Rome* 50.1: 85–99.

Recommended Works on Hannibal and the Punic Wars

Goldsworthy, A. 2001. *The Punic Wars*. Cassell Press.

Hanson, V. D. 2007. *Carnage and Culture: Landmark Battles in the Rise of Western Power*. Anchor Press, 99–134.

Hoyos, D. 2015. *Mastering the West: Rome and Carthage at War*. Oxford University Press.

Lancel, S. 1998. *Hannibal*. Blackwell Press.

Ancient Accounts of Hannibal and the Second Punic War

Appian. *Roman History*: Books 7 and 8 treat the Second and Third Punic Wars, respectively. [Transl. by H. White]. Available at http://www.livius.org/ap-ark/appian/appian_0.html

Eutropius. *Breviarium*: Books 2–4 treat the Punic Wars. [Transl. by J. S. Watson]. Available at http://www.tertullian.org/fathers/eutropius_breviarium_2_text.htm. There also exists a recent student edition of Book 3 by B. Beyer (2009. *War with Hannibal. Authentic Latin Prose for the Beginning Student*. Yale University Press).

Livy. *History of Rome*. Books 21–30 treat the Second Punic War [Transl. by C. Roberts]. Available at http://mcadams.posc.mu.edu/txt/ah/Livy/

Polybius. *Histories*. Book 1 treats the First Punic War; the Second Punic War and the simultaneous conflicts in the east are treated in Books 3–15 [Transl. by W. R. Paton]. Available at http://penelope.uchicago.edu/Thayer/E/Roman/Texts/Polybius/home.html

Silius Italicus, *Punica*: a lengthy Latin epic on the Second Punic War [Transl. by J. D. Duff]. Available at http://archive.org/stream/punicasi02siliuoft/punicasi02siliuoft_djvu.txt

Select Films, Documentaries, and Novels

Cabiria (1914): a feature–length Italian silent film; the title character was a Roman slave who narrowly escaped from the villainous Carthaginians during the Second Punic War. Available at http://youtu.be/gOWicOwtHa8

Scipio l'africano (1937): an account of Scipio's invasion of Africa, sponsored by Benito Mussolini. *Caveat spectator*: in the climactic Battle of Zama, several elephants are killed on screen. Available at http://youtu.be/6jjZ9U-4nN4

Jupiter's Darling (1955): a comedic musical; while Fabius Maximus delays, Hannibal is visited by his fiancée, Amytis.

Hannibal (1959): Hannibal falls in love with the fiancée of Fabius Maximus' son, before the Battle of Cannae. Not a first–rate film.

Engineering an Empire: Carthage (2006): an episode in the History Channel's series on ancient technology. An excellent source of reconstructions and short video clips on Carthaginian archaeology, battle tactics, and more. Excerpts available on YouTube.

Hannibal: Rome's Worst Nightmare (2006): a docudrama produced by the BBC; it focuses on Hannibal's Italy campaign. Available at http://www.youtube.com/watch?v=J1BKxeKtieM

On Hannibal's Trail (2012): a BBC documentary in which three Australian brothers bike Hannibal's route from Spain through Italy to Tunis.

Anderson, P. 2006 (new edn). "Delenda est" in the *Time Patrol* anthology. "Delenda Est" imagines an alternative history in which time travelers kill Scipio Africanus at the Battle of Ticinus, allowing Hannibal to annihilate Rome in 210 BCE.

Durham, David Anthony. 2006. *Pride of Carthage*. Anchor Press.

Flaubert, G. 1862. *Salammbo*, translated by A. J. Krailsheimer. Penguin Classics (1977). Flaubert's sensuous and sensational follow–up to *Madame Bovary*. The novel follows Salammbo, the daughter of Hamilcar Barca, as she becomes ensnared by the intrigues of the Mercenary War. Criticized by some as an indulgent exercise in Orientalism and imperialist propaganda, Flaubert's novel helped shape the image of Carthage in art and the popular imagination. Review essay by A. Mayor, 2010 available at http://www.stanford.edu/dept/HPS/MayorSweatingTruthCarth.pdf

Further Readings on Nepos and Ancient Biography

Beneker, J. 2009/2010. "Nepos' Biographical Method in the 'Lives of the Foreign Generals'". *Classical Journal* 105.2: 109–121.

Conte, G. B. 1994. *Latin Literature: A History*. The Johns Hopkins University Press, 221–223. Available at http://books.google.com/books?id=NJGp_dkXnuUC

Dionisotti, A. C. 1988. "Nepos and the Generals". *Journal of Roman Studies* 78: 35–49.

Elder, J. P. 1967. "Catullus I, His Poetic Creed, and Nepos". *Harvard Studies in Classical Philology* 71: 143–149.

Geiger, J. 1985. *Cornelius Nepos and Ancient Political Biography*. Franz Steiner Verglag.

Gibson, B. J. 1995. "Catullus 1.5–7". *Classical Quarterly* 45.2: 569–573.

Hallett, J. P. 2002. "Cornelius Nepos and Constructions of Gender in Augustan Poetry". In *Hommages à Carl Deroux* I: 254–256.

Horsfall, N. 1989. *Cornelius Nepos: A Selection, Including the Lives of Cato and Atticus*. Oxford University Press.

Jenkinson, E. 1967. "Nepos: An Introduction to Latin Biography". In T. A. Dorey (ed.), *Latin Biography*. Routledge and Kegan Paul, 1–15.

Marshall, P. K. 1977. *The Manuscript Tradition of Cornelius Nepos*. Institute of Classical Studies.

Millar, F. 1988. "Cornelius Nepos, Atticus and the Roman Revolution". *Greece and Rome* 35: 40–55.

Moles, J. L. 1989. "Nepos and Biography". *Classical Review* 39.2: 229–233.

Momigliano, A. D. *The Development of Greek Biography*. Harvard University Press, 96–104. http://books.google.com/books?id=9EVx6FI2D34C

Nipperdey, K., and K. Witte. 1913. *Cornelius Nepos*. Weidmann.

Rauk, J. 1996–1997. "Time and History in Catullus 1". *Classical World* 90.5: 319–332.

Stem, R. 2009–2010. "Shared Virtues and the Limits of Relativism in Nepos' Epaminondas and Atticus". *Classical Journal* 105.2: 123–136.

Tatum, W. J. 1997. "Friendship, Politics, and Literature in Catullus: Poems 1, 65 and 66, 116". *Classical Quarterly* 47: 482–500.

Tuplin, C. 2000. "Nepos and the Origin of Political Biography", in *Studies in Latin Literature and Roman History* X: 124–161. Available at https://www.academia.edu/8101855/Cornelius_Nepos_and_the_origins_of_political_biography

Wiseman, T. P. 1979. *Clio's Cosmetics: Three Studies in Greco–Roman Literature*. Rowman and Littlefield, 143–174. Available at http://books.google.com/books?id=xxitv2_FLhsC

Further Readings on Hannibal and the Punic Wars

Bagnall, N. 2002. *Essential Histories: The Punic Wars 264–146 BC*. Osprey Publishing.

Charles, M. B., and P. Rhodan. 2007. "'Magister Elephantorvm': A Reappraisal of Hannibal's Use of Elephants". *Classical World* 100.4: 363–389.

Daly, G. 2002. *Cannae: The Experience of Battle in the Second Punic War*. Routledge.

De Beer, G. 1969. *Hannibal: The Struggle for Power in the Mediterranean*. Thames & Hudson.

Garland, R. 2010. *Hannibal*. Bristol Classical Press.

Goldsworthy, A. 2007. *Cannae: Hannibal's Greatest Victory*. Phoenix.

Hoyos, D. 2010. *A Companion to the Punic Wars*. Wiley–Blackwell. (In particular Chs. 13, 14, 16–18, and 27). http://books.google.com/books?id=DeHoLjPOtTUC

Hoyos, D. 2005. *Hannibal's Dynasty: Power and Politics in the Western Mediterranean, 247–183 BC*. Oxford University Press.

Lancel, S. 1995. *Carthage: A History*. Oxford University Press.

Lazenby, J. F. 1998. *Hannibal's War: A Military History of the Second Punic War*. University of Oklahoma Press.

Little, C. E. 1934. "The Authenticity and Form of Cato's Saying 'Carthago Delenda Est'". *Classical Journal* 29.6: 429–435.

O'Connell, R. 2010. *The Ghosts of Cannae: Hannibal and the Darkest Hour of the Roman Republic*. Random House.

Palmer, R. 1997. *Rome and Carthage at Peace*. Fritz Steiner Verlag.

Peddie, J. 1997. *Hannibal's War*. Phoenix Mill. [lavishly illustrated]

Rich, J. 1996. "The Origins of the First and Second Punic Wars", in T. Cornell, B. Rankov, and P. Sabin (eds.), *The Second Punic War: A Reappraisal*. Institute of Classical Studies, 1–37.

Rosenstein, N. 2012. *Rome and the Mediterranean 290 to 146 BC: The Imperial Republic*. Edinburgh University Press.

Wise, T. 1982. *Armies of the Carthaginian Wars 265–146*. Osprey Publishing.

Chronology of Hannibal's Life

Date	Event	Nepos
ca. 247 BC	Birth of Hannibal. Hamilcar fights the Romans in Sicily.	
241	Rome defeats Carthaginian fleet at Aegates Islands. Carthage sues for peace, ending the First Punic War.	
241–237	Mercenary or Truceless War. Hamilcar leads the loyal resistance.	
237	Hannibal joins his father, Hamilcar, on campaign in Hispania.	Ch. 2
229	Hamilcar killed in battle. His son–in–law Hasdrubal the Fair assumes command of Carthaginian forces in Hispania. Romans active in Illyria.	Ch. 3.1
225	Romans sign Ebro treaty with Hasdrubal.	
224–222	Romans pacify the Gallic tribes of northern Italy.	
221	Hasdrubal the Fair assassinated. Hannibal proclaimed as leader of Carthaginian forces in Hispania. Philip V ascends to Macedonian throne.	
220	Hannibal's campaign against Vaccaei worries Romans. Romans demand that he respect Ebro treay. Construction of the Via Flaminia, which improved transportation from Rome to northern Italy and Illyria.	
219	Saguntum besieged and captured by Carthaginians, leading to outbreak of Second Punic War between Carthage and Rome. Rome embroiled in Second Illyrian War.	

© Bret Mulligan, CC BY 4.0   http://dx.doi.org/10.11647/OBP.0068.05

Date	Event	Nepos
218	Hannibal leads army across Alps into Italy. Romans defeated at Ticinus and Trebia. Carthaginian fleet raids Italy.	Ch. 3.4 Ch. 4
217	Roman army destroyed at Trasimene. Fabius Maximus elected dictator. Gnaeus and Publius Scipio win victories in Hispania. Hannibal nearly destroys the army of Minucius Rufus at Gerontium. Hannibal eludes Fabius in the Ager Falernus. Servilius raids Africa.	Ch. 5
216	Two Roman armies annihilated at Cannae. Another is destroyed in Gaul. Capua and many regions of southern Italy defect to Hannibal. Hannibal repulsed from Nola. Furius raids Africa.	
215	Hannibal's repeated attempts to take Nola are repulsed (215–214). He captures Casilinum. Bomilcar lands Carthaginian reinforcements in southern Italy. Gnaeus and Publius Scipio defeat Hasdrubal in Hispania. Otacilius raids Africa. A Carthaginian invasion of Sicily is thwarted by an outbreak of plague. Hannibal forges an alliance with Philip V of Macedon (First Macedonian War). Romans raid Carthaginian territory in Hispania.	
214	Romans recapture Casilinum. Hannibal fails to capture Tarentum. An army under his lieutenant Hanno destroyed at Beneventum. Syracuse defects to Carthage.	
213	Romans raise an army of over 200,000 men. They besiege Syracuse. Carthage attempts to reinforce Syracuse. Romans recapture Saguntum.	
212	Hannibal captures Tarentum and other cities in southern Italy. Roman army defeated at Silarus. Romans under Marcellus capture Syracuse. Capua besieged by Romans. Major battles at Lucania and Herdonea in Italy.	
211	Hannibal advances on Rome but is unable to capture city. Capua falls to Romans. In Hispania, Hasdrubal routs the armies of Gnaeus and Publius Scipio in the battles of the Upper Baetis. Major battles at Volturnus and Anio in Italy. Rome forges alliance with Aetolian League in Greece.	
210	Roman army destroyed at Herdonea. Scipio Africanus, aged 25, appointed leader of Roman forces in Hispania. Battles of Numistro and Venusia in Italy. Roman completes re–conquest of Sicily. Rome resumes raids in Africa.	

Chronology of Hannibal's Life

Date	Event	Nepos
209	Twelve Latin cities refuse to supply troops to Rome. Fabius recaptures Tarentum. Battle of Canusium. Scipio captures New Carthage. Philip defeats Aetolians at Lamia. Carthaginian fleet operates in Greek waters.	
208	Consuls Claudius Marcellus and Quinctius Crispinus ambushed and killed. Scipio defeats Hasdrubal at Baecula. Hasdrubal moves into Italy. Romans begin raiding African coast. Carthaginian fleet abandons Greece; another fleet defeated off Africa.	
207	Attempt to reinforce Hannibal by land fails when Hasdrubal is killed at Metaurus. Hannibal retreats into far southern Italy.	
206	Scipio annihilates a Carthaginian army at Ilipa, completing the conquest of Hispania. Romans campaign in Bruttium. Philip makes peace with Aetolians.	
205	Romans capture Locri. Philip V of Macedon negotiates a separate peace with Rome (Peace of Phoenike). Mago campaigns in northern Italy. Scipio elected consul.	
204	Continuing operations in Bruttium. Scipio begins offensive operations in northern Africa, besieges Utica, burns Carthaginian camp.	
203	Mago defeated in northern Italy; dies on route to Carthage. Carthaginians defeated at Great Plains in Africa. After Battle of Croton, Carthage sues for peace and Hannibal is recalled to Africa.	
202	Hannibal defeated at Battle of Zama by Scipio.	Ch. 6.3–4
201	Uneasy peace sworn between Rome and Carthage.	Ch. 7.1–5
196	Hannibal elected to head Carthaginian government.	
195–194	Hannibal flees to Crete and then to the court of King Antiochus III in Syria.	Ch. 7.6, Ch. 8.4
191–190	Romans defeat Antiochus at Thermopylae and Magnesia. Hannibal defeated in the Battle of Eurymedon. Hannibal flees to the court of King Prusias of Bithynia.	Ch. 9–11
ca.183	Hannibal commits suicide in Bithynia. Death of Scipio Africanus.	Ch. 12

Text of Nepos' *Life of Hannibal*

Prologus

(1) Nōn dubitō fore plērōsque, Attice, quī hoc genus scrīptūrae leve et nōn satis dīgnum summōrum virōrum persōnīs iūdicent, cum relātum legent, quis mūsicam docuerit Epamīnōndam, aut in ēius virtūtibus commemorārī saltāsse eum commodē scienterque tībiīs cantāsse.

(2) Sed hī erunt ferē, quī expertēs litterārum Graecārum nihil rēctum, nisi quod ipsōrum mōribus conveniat, putābunt.

(3) Hī sī didicerint nōn eadem omnibus esse honesta atque turpia, sed omnia maiōrum īnstitūtīs iūdicārī, nōn admīrābuntur nōs in Grāiōrum virtūtibus expōnendīs mōrēs eōrum secūtōs.

(4) Neque enim Cīmōnī fuit turpe, Athēniēnsium summō virō, sorōrem germānam habēre in mātrimōniō, quippe cum cīvēs ēius eōdem ūterentur īnstitūtō. At id quidem nostrīs mōribus nefās habētur. Laudī in Crētā dūcitur adulēscentulīs quam plūrimōs habuisse amātōrēs. Nūlla Lacedaemonī vidua tam est nōbilis, quae nōn †ad cēnam† eat mercēde conducta.

(5) Magnīs in laudibus tōtā ferē fuit Graeciā victōrem Olympiae citārī; in scaenam vērō prōdīre ac populō esse spectāculō nēminī in eīsdem gentibus fuit turpitūdinī. Quae omnia apud nōs partim īnfāmia, partim humilia atque ab honestāte remōta pōnuntur.

(6) Contrā ea plēraque nostrīs mōribus sunt decōra, quae apud illōs turpia putantur. Quem enim Rōmānōrum pudet uxōrem dūcere in convīvium?

Aut cuius nōn māter familiās prīmum locum tenet aedium atque in celēbritāte versātur?

(7) Quod multō fit aliter in Graeciā. Nam neque in convīvium adhibētur nisi propinquōrum, neque sedet nisi in interiōre parte aedium, quae gynaecōnītis appellātur; quō nēmō accēdit nisi propinquā cognātiōne coniūnctus.

(8) Sed hīc plūra persequī cum magnitūdō volūminis prohibet tum festīnātiō, ut ea explicem, quae exōrsus sum. Quārē ad prōpositum veniēmus et in hōc expōnēmus librō dē vītā excellentium imperātōrum.

Listen to the *Prologus* read by Christopher Francese
http://dx.doi.org/10.11647/OBP.0068.09

Chapter 1

(1) Hannibal, Hamilcaris fīlius, Karthāginiēnsis. Sī vērum est, quod nēmō dubitat, ut populus Rōmānus omnēs gentēs virtūte superārit, nōn est īnfitiandum Hannibalem tantō praestitisse cēterōs imperātōrēs prūdentiā, quantō populus Rōmānus antecēdat fortitūdine cūnctās nātiōnēs.

(2) Nam quotiēnscumque cum eō congressus est in Italiā, semper discessit superior. Quod nisi domī cīvium suōrum invidiā dēbilitātus esset, Rōmānōs vidētur superāre potuisse. Sed multōrum obtrectātiō dēvīcit ūnīus virtūtem.

(3) Hic autem, velut hērēditāte relictum, odium paternum ergā Rōmānōs sīc cōnservāvit, ut prius animam quam id dēposuerit, quī quidem, cum patriā pulsus esset et aliēnārum opum indigēret, numquam dēstiterit animō bellāre cum Rōmānīs.

Listen to chapter 1 read by Christopher Francese
http://dx.doi.org/10.11647/OBP.0068.10

Chapter 2

(1) Nam ut omittam Philippum, quem absēns hostem reddidit Rōmānīs, omnium iīs temporibus potentissimus rēx Antiochus fuit. Hunc tantā cupiditāte incendit bellandī, ut ūsque ā rubrō marī arma cōnātus sit īnferre Italiae.

(2) Ad quem cum lēgātī vēnissent Rōmānī, quī dē ēius voluntāte explōrārent darentque operam, cōnsiliīs clandestīnīs, ut Hannibalem in suspīciōnem rēgī addūcerent, tamquam ab ipsīs corruptus alia atque anteā sentīret, neque id frūstrā fēcissent idque Hannibal comperisset sēque ab interiōribus cōnsiliīs sēgregārī vīdisset, tempore datō adiit ad rēgem.

(3) Eīque cum multa dē fidē suā et odiō in Rōmānōs commemorāsset, hoc adiūnxit: "Pater meus" inquit "Hamilcar puerulō mē, utpote nōn amplius novem annōs nātō, in Hispāniam imperātor proficīscēns, Karthāgine Iovī optimō maximō hostiās immolāvit.

(4) Quae dīvīna rēs dum cōnficiēbātur, quaesīvit ā mē, vellemne sēcum in castra proficīscī. Id cum libenter accēpissem atque ab eō petere coepissem, nē dubitāret dūcere, tum ille 'Faciam', inquit 'sī mihi fidem, quam postulō, dederis.' Simul mē ad āram addūxit, apud quam sacrificāre īnstituerat, eamque cēterīs remōtīs tenentem iūrāre iūssit numquam mē in amīcitiā cum Rōmānīs fore.

(5) Id ego iūs iūrandum patrī datum ūsque ad hanc aetātem ita cōnservāvī, ut nēminī dubium esse dēbeat, quīn reliquō tempore eādem mente sim futūrus.

(6) Quārē, sī quid amīcē dē Rōmānīs cōgitābis, nōn imprūdenter fēceris, sī mē cēlāris; cum quidem bellum parābis, tē ipsum frūstrāberis, sī nōn mē in eō prīncipem posueris.

Listen to chapter 2 read by Christopher Francese
http://dx.doi.org/10.11647/OBP.0068.11

Chapter 3

(1) Hāc igitur, quā dīximus, aetāte cum patre in Hispāniam profectus est. Cuius post obitum, Hasdrubale imperātōre suffectō, equitātuī omnī praefuit. Hōc quoque interfectō, exercitus summam imperiī ad eum dētulit. Id Karthāginem dēlātum pūblicē comprobātum est.

(2) Sīc Hannibal, minor quīnque et vīgintī annīs nātus imperātor factus, proximō trienniō omnēs gentēs Hispāniae bellō subēgit; Saguntum, foederātam cīvitātem, vī expugnāvit; trēs exercitūs maximōs comparāvit.

(3) Ex hīs ūnum in Āfricam mīsit, alterum cum Hasdrubale frātre in Hispāniā relīquit, tertium in Italiam sēcum dūxit. Saltum Pȳrēnaeum trānsiit. Quācumque iter fēcit, cum omnibus incolīs cōnflīxit: nēminem nisi victum dīmīsit.

(4) Ad Alpēs posteāquam vēnit, quae Italiam ab Galliā sēiungunt, quās nēmō umquam cum exercitū ante eum praeter Herculem Grāium trānsierat, quō factō is hodiē saltus Grāius appellātur, Alpicōs cōnantēs prohibēre trānsitū concīdit; loca patefēcit, itinera mūniit, effēcit, ut eā elephantus ōrnātus īre posset, quā anteā ūnus homō inermis vix poterat rēpere. Hāc cōpiās trādūxit in Italiamque pervēnit.

> 🔊 Listen to chapter 3 read by Christopher Francese
> http://dx.doi.org/10.11647/OBP.0068.12

Chapter 4

(1) Cōnflīxerat apud Rhodanum cum P. Cornēliō Scīpiōne cōnsule eumque pepulerat. Cum hōc eōdem Clastidī apud Padum dēcernit sauciumque inde ac fugātum dīmittit.

(2) Tertiō īdem Scīpiō cum collēgā Tiberiō Longō apud Trebiam adversus eum vēnit. Cum hīs manum cōnseruit, utrōsque prōflīgāvit. Inde per Ligurēs Appennīnum trānsiit, petēns Etrūriam.

(3) Hōc itinere adeō gravī morbō adficitur oculōrum, ut posteā numquam dextrō aequē bene ūsus sit. Quā valētūdine cum etiam tum premerētur lectīcāque ferrētur, C. Flāminium cōnsulem apud Trasumēnum cum exercitū īnsidiīs circumventum occīdit, neque multō post C. Centēnium praetōrem cum dēlēctā manū saltūs occupantem. Hinc in Āpuliam pervēnit.

(4) Ibi obviam eī vēnērunt duo cōnsulēs, C. Terentius et L. Aemilius. Utrīusque exercitūs ūnō proeliō fugāvit, Paulum cōnsulem occīdit et aliquot praetereā cōnsulārēs, in hīs Cn. Servīlium Geminum, quī superiōre annō fuerat cōnsul.

Listen to chapter 4 read by Christopher Francese
http://dx.doi.org/10.11647/OBP.0068.13

Chapter 5

(1) Hāc pugnā pugnātā, Rōmam profectus nūllō resistente. In propinquīs urbī montibus morātus est. Cum aliquot ibi diēs castra habuisset et Capuam reverterētur, Q. Fabius Māximus, dictātor Rōmānus, in agrō Falernō eī sē obiēcit.

(2) Hic, clausus locōrum angustiīs, noctū sine ūllō dētrīmentō exercitūs sē expedīvit; Fabiōque, callidissimō imperātōrī, dedit verba. Namque, obductā nocte, sarmenta in cornibus iuvencōrum dēligāta incendit ēiusque generis multitūdinem magnam dispālātam immīsit. Quō repentīnō obiectō vīsū tantum terrōrem iniēcit exercituī Rōmānōrum, ut ēgredī extrā vāllum nēmō sit ausus.

(3) Hanc post rem gestam nōn ita multīs diēbus M. Minucium Rūfum, magistrum equitum parī ac dictātōrem imperiō, dolō prōductum in proelium, fugāvit. Ti. Semprōnium Gracchum, iterum cōnsulem, in Lūcānīs absēns in īnsidiās inductum sustulit. M. Claudium Marcellum, quīnquiēns cōnsulem, apud Venusiam parī modō interfēcit.

(4) Longum est omnia ēnumerāre proelia. Quā rē hoc ūnum satis erit dictum, ex quō intellegī possit, quantus ille fuerit: quamdiū in Italiā fuit, nēmō eī in aciē restitit, nēmō adversus eum post Cannēnsem pugnam in campō castra posuit.

Listen to chapter 5 read by Christopher Francese
http://dx.doi.org/10.11647/OBP.0068.14

Chapter 6

(1) Hinc invictus patriam dēfēnsum revocātus, bellum gessit adversus P. Scīpiōnem, filium ēius, quem ipse prīmō apud Rhodanum, iterum apud Padum, tertiō apud Trebiam fugārat.

(2) Cum hōc, exhaustīs iam patriae facultātibus, cupīvit impraesentiārum bellum compōnere, quō valentior posteā congrederētur. In colloquium convēnit; condiciōnēs nōn convēnērunt.

(3) Post id factum paucīs diēbus apud Zamam cum eōdem cōnflīxit: pulsus — incrēdibile dictū — bīduō et duābus noctibus Hadrūmētum pervēnit, quod abest ab Zamā circiter mīlia passuum trecenta.

(4) In hāc fugā, Numidae, quī simul cum eō ex aciē excesserant, īnsidiātī sunt eī; quōs nōn sōlum effūgit, sed etiam ipsōs oppressit. Hadrūmētī reliquōs ē fugā collēgit; novīs dīlēctibus paucīs diēbus multōs contrāxit.

Listen to chapter 6 read by Christopher Francese
http://dx.doi.org/10.11647/OBP.0068.15

Chapter 7

(1) Cum in apparandō ācerrimē esset occupātus, Karthāginiēnsēs bellum cum Rōmānīs composuērunt. Ille nihilō sētius exercituī posteā praefuit rēsque in Āfricā gessit ūsque ad P. Sulpicium C. Aurēlium cōnsulēs.

(2) Hīs enim magistrātibus lēgātī Karthāginiēnsēs Rōmam vēnērunt, quī senātuī populōque Rōmānō grātiās agerent, quod cum iīs pācem fēcissent, ob eamque rem corōnā aureā eōs dōnārent, simulque peterent ut obsidēs eōrum Fregellīs essent captīvīque redderentur.

(3) Hīs ex senātūs cōnsultō respōnsum est: mūnus eōrum grātum acceptumque esse; obsidēs, quō locō rogārent, futūrōs; captīvōs nōn remissūrōs, quod Hannibalem, cuius operā susceptum bellum foret, inimīcissimum nōminī Rōmānō, etiam nunc cum imperiō apud exercitum habērent itemque frātrem ēius Māgōnem.

(4) Hōc respōnsō Karthāginiēnsēs cognitō, Hannibalem domum et Māgōnem revocārunt. Hūc ut rediit, rēx factus est, postquam praetor fuerat annō secundō et vīcēsimō. Ut enim Rōmae cōnsulēs, sīc Karthāgine quotannīs annuī bīnī rēgēs creābantur.

(5) In eō magistrātū parī dīligentiā sē Hannibal praebuit, ac fuerat in bellō. Namque effēcit, ex novīs vectīgālibus nōn sōlum ut esset pecūnia, quae Rōmānīs ex foedere penderētur, sed etiam superesset, quae in aerāriō repōnerētur.

(6) Deinde M. Claudiō L. Fūriō cōnsulibus, Rōmā lēgātī Karthāginem vēnērunt. Hōs Hannibal ratus suī exposcendī grātiā missōs, priusquam iīs senātus darētur, nāvem ascendit clam atque in Syriam ad Antiochum perfūgit.

(7) Hāc rē palam factā Poenī nāvēs duās, quae eum comprehenderent, sī possent cōnsequī, mīsērunt, bona ēius pūblicārunt, domum ā fundāmentīs disiēcērunt, ipsum exsulem iūdicārunt.

Listen to chapter 7 read by Christopher Francese
http://dx.doi.org/10.11647/OBP.0068.16

Chapter 8

(1) At Hannibal annō tertiō, postquam domō profūgerat, L. Cornēliō Q. Minuciō cōnsulibus, cum quīnque nāvibus Āfricam accessit in fīnibus Cȳrēnaeōrum, sī forte Karthāginiēnsēs ad bellum Antiochī spē fīdūciāque

indūcere posset, cui iam persuāserat, ut cum exercitibus in Italiam proficīscerētur. Hūc Māgōnem frātrem excīvit.

(2) Id ubi Poenī rēscīvērunt, Māgōnem eādem, quā frātrem, absentem affēcērunt poenā. Illī, dēspērātīs rēbus, cum solvissent nāvēs ac vēla ventīs dedissent, Hannibal ad Antiochum pervēnit. Dē Māgōnis interitū duplex memoria prōdita est. Namque aliī naufragiō, aliī ā servulīs ipsīus interfectum eum scrīptum relīquērunt.

(3) Antiochus autem, sī tam in agendō bellō cōnsiliīs ēius pārēre voluisset, quam in suscipiendō īnstituerat, propius Tiberī quam Thermopylīs dē summā imperiī dīmicāsset. Quem etsī multa stultē cōnārī vidēbat, tamen nūllā dēseruit in rē.

(4) Praefuit paucīs nāvibus, quās ex Syriā iussus erat in Āsiam dūcere, iīsque adversus Rhodiōrum classem in Pamphȳliō marī cōnflīxit. Quō cum multitūdine adversāriōrum suī superārentur, ipse, quō cornū rem gessit, fuit superior.

🔊 Listen to chapter 8 read by Christopher Francese
http://dx.doi.org/10.11647/OBP.0068.17

Chapter 9

(1) Antiochō fugātō, verēns nē dēderētur, quod sine dubiō accidisset, sī suī fēcisset potestātem, Crētam ad Gortȳniōs vēnit, ut ibi, quō sē cōnferret, cōnsīderāret.

(2) Vīdit autem vir omnium callidissimus in magnō sē fore perīculō, nisi quid prōvīdisset, propter avāritiam Crētēnsium. Magnam enim sēcum pecūniam portābat, dē quā sciēbat exīsse fāmam.

(3) Itaque capit tāle cōnsilium. Amphorās complūrēs complet plumbō, summās operit aurō et argentō. Hās, praesentibus prīncipibus, dēpōnit in templō Diānae, simulāns sē suās fortūnās illōrum fideī crēdere. Hīs in errōrem inductīs, statuās aēneās, quās sēcum portābat, omnī suā pecūniā complet eāsque in prōpatulō domī abicit.

(4) Gortȳniī templum magnā cūrā custōdiunt, nōn tam ā cēterīs quam ab Hannibale, nē ille, īnscientibus iīs, tolleret sēcumque dūceret.

Listen to chapter 9 read by Christopher Francese
http://dx.doi.org/10.11647/OBP.0068.18

Chapter 10

(1) Sīc cōnservātīs suīs rēbus, Poenus, illūsīs Crētēnsibus omnibus, ad Prūsiam in Pontum pervēnit. Apud quem eōdem animō fuit ergā Italiam neque aliud quicquam ēgit quam rēgem armāvit et exercuit adversus Rōmānōs.

(2) Quem cum vidēret domesticīs opibus minus esse rōbustum, conciliābat cēterōs rēgēs, adiungēbat bellicōsās nātiōnēs. Dissidēbat ab eō Pergamēnus rēx Eumenēs, Rōmānīs amīcissimus, bellumque inter eōs gerēbātur et marī et terrā.

(3) Sed utrobīque Eumenēs plūs valēbat propter Rōmānōrum societātem. Quō magis cupiēbat eum Hannibal opprimī; quem sī remōvisset, faciliōra sibi cētera fore arbitrābātur. Ad hunc interficiendum tālem iniit ratiōnem.

(4) Classe paucīs diēbus erant dēcrētūrī. Superābātur nāvium multitūdine; dolō erat pugnandum, cum pār nōn esset armīs. Imperāvit quam plūrimās venēnātās serpentēs vīvās colligī eāsque in vāsa fictilia conicī.

(5) Hārum cum effēcisset magnam multitūdinem, diē ipsō, quō factūrus erat nāvāle proelium, classiāriōs convocat iīsque praecipit, omnēs ut in ūnam Eumenis rēgis concurrant nāvem, ā cēterīs tantum satis habeant sē dēfendere. Id illōs facile serpentium multitūdine cōnsecūtūrōs.

(6) Rēx autem in quā nāve veherētur, ut scīrent, sē factūrum. Quem sī aut cēpissent aut interfēcissent, magnō iīs pollicētur praemiō fore.

Listen to chapter 10 read by Christopher Francese
http://dx.doi.org/10.11647/OBP.0068.19

Chapter 11

(1) Tālī cohortātiōne mīlitum factā, classis ab utrīsque in proelium dēdūcitur. Quārum aciē cōnstitūtā, priusquam signum pugnae darētur, Hannibal, ut palam faceret suīs, quō locō Eumenēs esset, tabellārium in scaphā cum cādūceō mittit.

(2) Quī ubi ad nāvēs adversāriōrum pervēnit epistulamque ostendēns, sē rēgem professus est quaerere, statim ad Eumenem dēductus est, quod nēmō dubitābat, quīn aliquid dē pāce esset scrīptum. Tabellārius, ducis nāve dēclārātā suīs, eōdem, unde erat ēgressus, sē recēpit.

(3) At Eumenēs, solūtā epistulā, nihil in eā repperit, nisi quae ad irrīdendum eum pertinērent. Cuius etsī causam mīrābātur neque reperiēbat, tamen proelium statim committere nōn dubitāvit.

(4) Hōrum in concursū Bīthȳniī Hannibalis praeceptō ūniversī nāvem Eumenis adoriuntur. Quōrum vim rēx cum sustinēre nōn posset, fugā salūtem petiit; quam cōnsecūtus nōn esset, nisi intrā sua praesidia sē recēpisset, quae in proximō lītore erant conlocāta.

(5) Reliquae Pergamēnae nāvēs cum adversāriōs premerent ācrius, repente in eās vāsa fictilia, dē quibus suprā mentiōnem fēcimus, conicī coepta sunt. Quae iacta initiō rīsum pugnantibus concitārunt, neque, quā rē id fieret, poterat intellegī.

(6) Postquam autem nāvēs suās opplētās cōnspexērunt serpentibus, novā rē perterritī, cum, quid potissimum vītārent, nōn vidērent, puppēs vertērunt sēque ad sua castra nautica rettulērunt.

(7) Sīc Hannibal cōnsiliō arma Pergamēnōrum superāvit, neque tum sōlum, sed saepe aliās pedestribus cōpiīs parī prūdentiā pepulit adversāriōs.

Listen to chapter 11 read by Christopher Francese
http://dx.doi.org/10.11647/OBP.0068.20

Chapter 12

(1) Quae dum in Āsia geruntur, accidit cāsū, ut lēgātī Prūsiae Rōmae apud T. Quīnctium Flāminīnum cōnsulārem cēnārent, atque ibi dē Hannibale mentiōne factā, ex iīs ūnus dīceret eum in Prūsiae rēgnō esse.

(2) Id posterō diē Flāminīnus senātuī dētulit. Patrēs cōnscrīptī, quī Hannibale vīvō numquam sē sine īnsidiīs futūrōs existimārent, lēgātōs in Bīthȳniam mīsērunt, in iīs Flāminīnum, quī ab rēge peterent, nē inimīcissimum suum sēcum habēret sibique dēderet.

(3) Hīs Prūsias negāre ausus nōn est: illud recūsāvit, nē id ā sē fierī postulārent, quod adversus iūs hospitiī esset; ipsī, sī possent, comprehenderent; locum, ubi esset, facile inventūrōs. Hannibal enim ūnō locō sē tenēbat, in castellō, quod eī ā rēge datum erat mūnerī, idque sīc aedificārat, ut in omnibus partibus aedificiī exitūs habēret, scīlicet verēns, nē ūsū venīret, quod accidit.

(4) Hūc cum lēgātī Rōmānōrum vēnissent ac multitūdine domum ēius circumdedissent, puer, ab iānuā prōspiciēns, Hannibalī dīxit plūrēs praeter cōnsuētūdinem armātōs appārēre. Quī imperāvit eī, ut omnēs forēs aedificiī circumīret ac properē sibi nūntiāret, num eōdem modō undique obsidērētur.

(5) Puer cum celeriter, quid esset, renūntiāsset omnīsque exitūs occupātōs ostendisset, sēnsit id nōn fortuītō factum, sed sē petī neque sibi diūtius vītam esse retinendam. Quam nē aliēnō arbitriō dīmitteret, memor prīstinārum virtūtum, venēnum, quod semper sēcum habēre cōnsuērat, sūmpsit.

Listen to chapter 12 read by Christopher Francese
http://dx.doi.org/10.11647/OBP.0068.21

Chapter 13

(1) Sīc vir fortissimus, multīs variīsque perfūnctus labōribus, annō acquiēvit septuāgēsimō. Quibus cōnsulibus interierit, nōn convēnit. Namque Atticus M. Claudiō Marcellō Q. Fabiō Labeōne cōnsulibus mortuum in Annālī suō scrīptum relīquit, at Polybius L. Aemiliō Paulō Cn. Baebiō Tamphilō, Sulpicius autem Blithō P. Cornēliō Cethēgō M. Baebiō Tamphilō.

(2) Atque hic tantus vir tantīsque bellīs districtus nōn nihil temporis tribuit litterīs. Namque aliquot ēius librī sunt, Graecō sermōne cōnfectī, in iīs ad Rhodiōs dē Cn. Manliī Volsōnis in Āsiā rēbus gestīs.

(3) Huius bellī gesta multī memoriae prōdidērunt, sed ex iīs duo, quī cum eō in castrīs fuērunt simulque vīxērunt, quam diū fortūna passa est, Sīlēnus et Sōsylus Lacedaemonius. Atque hōc Sōsylō Hannibal litterārum Graecārum ūsus est doctōre.

(4) Sed nōs tempus est huius librī facere fīnem et Rōmānōrum explicāre imperātōrēs, quō facilius, collātīs utrōrumque factīs, quī virī praeferendī sint, possit iūdicārī.

Listen to chapter 13 read by Christopher Francese
http://dx.doi.org/10.11647/OBP.0068.22

Notes

Prologus

Nepos introduces his collection of biographies of famous generals.

(1) nōn dubitō fore plērōsque: indirect statement with a verb of expecting (AG §580c),[1] "I do not doubt that there will be a great many (people)". **fore:** alternative form of *futūrōs esse*.

Attice: Nepos' friend, Titus Pomponius Atticus (ca. 109–ca. 32 BC). The vocative signals that the work is dedicated to him. Atticus was a wealthy and learned man who spent many years living in Greece, thus earning him the agnomen "the man from Athens". From the letters of Cicero, with whom Atticus maintained a lifelong correspondence, we know that Atticus occasionally returned to Rome and was involved in various political negotiations and affairs on Cicero's behalf. Atticus' house on the Quirinal hill in Rome often served as a meeting place for writers such as Nepos, Cicero, and the greatest scholar of the age, Marcus Terentius Varro. In addition to an influential epitome of Roman history (*Liber annalis*), he composed letters, poetry, and an account of Cicero's consulship in Greek. None of Atticus' works have survived.

quī...iūdicent: relative clause of characteristic (AG §535); its antecedent is *plērōsque*.

leve: "unimportant, trivial", in comparison to more serious genres, such as history.

dīgnum: "worthy of" + ablative (AG §418b).

---

1 The references in round brackets that occur throughout this chapter point to *Allen and Greenough's New Latin Grammar*, available at the Dickinson Classics website, http://dcc.dickinson.edu/allen-greenough/

cum relātum legent: "when they (will) read it related/told". *relātum* is the perfect passive participle of *referō*.

quis mūsicam docuerit Epamīnōndam: indirect question with perfect subjunctive, *docuerit* (AG §574). An educated Greek man was expected to be able to play the lyre and sing festive, improvised songs known as *skolia* at dinner parties. Romans thought such behavior beneath the dignity of a freeborn male.

    docuerit: *doceō* takes a double accusative of the person taught (*Epamīnōndam*) and the subject being taught (*mūsicam*).

    Epamīnōndam: Epaminondas, a Theban general and statesman, was hailed in antiquity as one of the most virtuous and incorruptible of the Greeks. Nepos' biography of Epaminondas, who forever broke Sparta's military power at the Battle of Leuctra (371 BC), survives.

ēius...eum: i.e., Epaminondas.

commemorārī: passive infinitive dependent on *relātum legent* and introducing two indirect statements that describe the other un–Roman activities performed by Epaminondas, 1) *saltāsse eum commodē* and 2) *scienterque tībiīs cantāsse*.

saltā(vi)sse and **cantā(vi)sse:** syncopated perfects (AG §181).

(2) hī: referring back to the *plērōsque* in the previous sentence; antecedent of *quī*, "those who...".

ferē: with words of number or quantity (e.g., *plērōsque*), "for the most part".

expertēs: in apposition with *quī*. *expers* takes the genitive, *litterārum Graecārum*, "ignorant of Greek culture". Remember that *expers* is derived from *ex–pars* ("to have no part in"); it should not be confused with "expert", derived from *expertus > experior* ("to try, to have experienced").

nisi quod: "except that which...", introducing a relative clause of characteristic.

mōribus: "ways" or "customs", dative with the compound verb, *conveniat*.

(3) didicerint: future perfect > *discō*, introducing an indirect statement.

turpia: "ugly" in the sense of "morally reprehensible". This is a key word for Nepos in the *Prologus*.

maiōrum: "of (their own) ancestors".

nōs... secūtōs [esse]: indirect statement dependent on *nōn admīrābuntur*. **nōs:** i.e., Nepos; ancient authors often referred to themselves using plural forms, especially in prose. Although the precise connotation of this common usage is debatable, it does not convey haughtiness or pretension, as the use of English "we" might in a similar circumstance.

in Grāiōrum virtūtibus expōnendīs: "in setting forth the excellences of Greeks". **expōnendīs** is gerundive (AG §503). Nepos mentions Greeks because most of the foreigners in his biographies are Greek, but non–Greek foreign generals—Datames, Hamilcar, and Hannibal—are also treated with respect.

eōrum: i.e., *Grāiōrum*.

(4) enim: introduces an example that explains the generalization in the previous sentence.

Cīmōnī: Cimon, an Athenian general, played an important role in neutralizing Persia's threat to Greece in the aftermath of the Persian Wars (490–479 BC).

Athēniēnsium summō virō: in apposition with *Cīmōnī*.

sorōrem germānam: although *germānam* would usually indicate a full sibling, it can refer to a sister with the same father but a different mother. It is unclear whether Nepos means to imply that Cimon married his half–sister, which is true, or if he mistakenly believed that Cimon married his full sister. Marrying a full sister was generally considered taboo in Athens, although according to the Hellenistic Jewish philosopher Philo of Alexandria (ca. 20 BC–AD 50) an old law in Athens permitted men to marry their sisters by the same father, while the equivalent law in Sparta permitted men to marry sisters by the same mother, but not vice versa (Philo, *On Special Laws* 3.4). Following the analogy of seeds and soil in agriculture, most ancient Greeks and Romans subscribed to the theory that the male seed was the active element of reproduction.

quippe: intensifying affirmative particle emphasizing the causal *cum* clause (AG §549).

cīvēs: "fellow citizens".

ūterentur: "use" + ablative of means, *eōdem... īnstitūtō* (AG §410).

nostrīs mōribus: i.e., Roman customs.

nefās: something that is contrary to moral law or the dictates of heaven, "taboo".

laudī dūcitur adulēscentulīs: "it is considered a (source of) honor for young men". **laudī** is a dative of purpose in a double dative construction in which *adulēscentulīs* is the dative of reference (AG §382).

quam plūrimōs amātōrēs: "as many lovers as possible"; *quam* + superlative: "as...as possible" (AG §291c). Nepos here refers to relationships between older and younger men.

Lacedaemonī: locative, "in Sparta" (AG §35h).

nūlla vidua est quae: "there is no widow of the sort who...", introducing a relative clause of characteristic.

†ad cēnam† eat mercēde conducta: the meaning of this phrase is unclear and the text may be corrupt; other manuscripts read *ad scaenam* ("on stage") and scholars have offered numerous conjectures for what Nepos may have written (e.g., *obscena*, "lewdness, indecency"). No ancient author supports Nepos' contention that it was honorable for Spartan widows to hire themselves out as courtesans at feasts; nevertheless, since many ancient authors spoke about the moral laxity of Spartan woman, it is not difficult to imagine how such a misconception might arise.

eat: present subjunctive > *eō, īre*.

mercēde conducta: "hired for a fee"; *mercēde*: ablative of price (AG §416).

(5) tōtā... Graeciā: ablative of place where. When an adjective is used, the preposition *in* is often omitted, regularly so with *tōtus* (AG §429.2); compare *in Graeciā* (12.3).

victōrem Olympiae citārī: "to be announced as champion at Olympia".

populō esse spectāculō: "to be a (source of) spectacle for the people", double dative construction (AG §382).

nēminī fuit turpitūdinī: another double dative.

apud nōs: "among us", i.e., in Roman as opposed to Greek culture.

pōnuntur: "are considered"; Nepos frequently uses this verb as a synonym of *habeor, iūdicō,* or *exīstimō.*

(6) contrā ea: "in opposition to these things", i.e., "on the other hand"; *ea* (neuter plural) refers to the previous sentence. This phrase is common in prose writers of the late republic (e.g., Caesar and Livy).

nostrīs mōribus: dative with *decōra.*

quem: interrogative pronoun, accusative of the person affected by the sentiment of the impersonal verb, *pudet,* "it is shameful to which of the Romans…?"; i.e., "what Roman feels shame…?"

Rōmānōrum: partitive genitive limiting *quem* (AG §346).

uxōrem dūcere: "to lead [one's] wife" (rather than the common idiom, "to marry").

māter familiās: the loyal wife of the head of the Roman family, the *pater familias; familiās* is an old form of the first declension genitive (AG §43b). Nepos' comments about the free movement of Roman women should be taken to apply to upper class women in respectable households. While *pater familias* was a strictly defined legal term referring to the oldest male in a *familia,* the Roman jurist Ulpian (AD 170–228) claimed that "character is what distinguishes and separates a *mater familias* from other women; accordingly it makes no difference whether she is married or a widow, freeborn or freed; for neither marriage nor birth make a *mater familias,* but good character" (*Digest* 50.16.46.1). The strong association of the term with the sexual chastity of the respectable Roman *matrona* explains Nepos' use of the term in this context. Women of lower socio–economic status would, presumably, have even fewer constraints on their public visibility, although information about their lives is scanty.

prīmum locum: i.e., the atrium. Originally used for domestic industry such as weaving, it became the principle receiving room of the upper–class Roman house.

in celēbritāte versātur: "appears in public".

(7) quod: connective relative that associates the sentence with part or all of the preceding thought (AG §308f).

multō: "by a lot", "much" (modifying *aliter*); ablative of degree of difference (AG §414).

nisi propinquōrum: "except among relations".

quō: "(to) where", adverb modifying *accēdit*.

(8) hīc: adverbial, "at this point".

plūra persequī: "recounting more instances", an object clause (AG §452) explaining what the scope of the book (*magnitūdō volūminis*) and Nepos' eagerness (*festīnātiō*) prevent (*prohibet*).

cum...tum: "both...and...".

magnitūdō volūminis: could refer just to the book of biographies of foreign generals, or to the entire corpus of sixteen books, which contained over 400 biographies.

festīnātiō ut ea explicem, quae exōrsus sum: "my haste to explain those things (*ea*) which (*quae*)..."; *ut* introduces a purpose clause triggered by *festīnātiō*, a noun that contains the notion of action.

ad prōpositum: "to the point" (of the task).

veniēmus...expōnēmus: note the future tense.

Essay on Nepos' *Prologus* to the *Lives of Outstanding Commanders*

In this short preface to his biographies of foreign generals, Nepos dedicates the work to his friend Titus Pomponius Atticus (ca. 109–ca. 32 BC) and warns that his readers should not be shocked to see celebrated foreigners engaging in behavior that would seem scandalous or reprehensible if undertaken by a Roman. Customs differ between nations, he says, since they arise from different national traditions.

Nepos suggests that some readers may find this kind of writing trivial (*leve*), a remark that can be understood as referring to biography per se, or to the particular challenge of writing biographies of generals, whose exploits were traditionally told in the serious genre of history. Despite this gesture of modesty, Nepos does employ some devices of the higher genre of history writing proper. The rhythm of the opening phrase, for example, is dactylic, the meter of epic: *Nōn dŭbĭtō fŏrĕ plērōsque, Āttĭcĕ, quī hōc*. Many historians begin their prose works with such a poetic flourish (e.g. Livy, Eutropius, and Tacitus), and formal Latin prose generally includes moments of metrical rhythm, especially at the beginning and end of long periods.

To seek out the best lessons of noble conduct, Nepos decided that he would not limit his biographies to notable Romans, but would present the noble characters of Romans and foreigners alike. Evaluating the morality and virtue of foreigners, however, presented a challenge. Nepos imagines a chauvinistic response from those unable to take seriously people who engaged in activities that upper–class male Romans generally agreed were disgraceful—such as dancing, or appearing on stage for the entertainment of the common people, or keeping their women cloistered in the house— or even unlawful, like marrying a close relative.

While Nepos' tolerance of other cultural practices may strike the modern reader as refreshing, the differences in customs and behaviors mentioned by Nepos are ultimately shown to be superficial. Indeed, in Nepos' view, cultural difference is an illusion that masks the common nature of all people: "the nature of all states is the same" (*eandem omnium civitatum esse naturam*). A Greek might dance or play the flute or marry his half–sister; but all good men—Greek, Roman, or even Carthaginian— display the universal virtues of intelligence, courage, and loyalty, and so reveal themselves as suitable models for the behavior of even the most upright Roman reader.

Chapter 1

Nepos compares Hannibal's individual greatness to the superiority of the Roman people (1–2). Hannibal's implacable hostility towards the Romans, even after being sent into exile by his fellow–citizens, was a kind of family inheritance (3).

(1) Hannibal: Most Carthaginian proper names are rendered in Latin as third declension nouns. In Punic, the language spoken by the Carthaginians, Hannibal meant something like "The Favorite of Baal". Baal Hammon was the chief god of the Carthaginians.

Hamilcaris: Hamilcar (ca. 275–229 BC) was a Carthaginian general and father of three sons: Hannibal, Hasdrubal, and Mago, all of whom led armies against Rome in the Second Punic War. In the latter phase of the First Punic War (264–241 BC), Hamilcar waged a brilliant guerilla campaign to defend

Mount Hercte and Mount Eryx in Sicily. His aptitude for quick, devastating raids earned him the nickname Barca or "Thunderbolt". Hamilcar so impressed the Romans with his ferocity and ingenuity that, when Carthage surrendered, Hamilcar and his soldiers were allowed to keep their weapons, a symbol that they were never defeated. Nepos recounts these exploits in the first chapter of his *Life of Hamilcar*. Before Hamilcar died in battle in 229 BC, he conquered extensive territory in Hispania and founded the city of Barcino (modern Barcelona).

Karthāginiēnsis: Adjectives ending in *–ēnsis* indicate a person or thing that belongs to something or comes from someplace (AG §249).

sī vērum est: indicative because Nepos believes that his statement is true. He further emphasizes its veracity with the relative clause, *quod nēmō dubitat*.

ut populus Rōmānus omnēs gentēs virtūte superārit: substantive clause that articulates what is *vērum* (AG §571c).
   virtūte: ablative of specification, revealing the quality in which the *populus Rōmānus* surpasses *omnēs gentēs* (AG §418). Nepos refers to the Romans' military aptitude, not their "virtue" in general. Nepos' general stance, articulated in the *Prologus* to the *Lives of Outstanding Commanders*, is that no single people has a monopoly on virtue.
   superārit: = *superā(ve)rit*, syncopated perfect (AG §181).

nōn est īnfitiandum: future passive periphrastic indicating necessity or obligation (AG §500.2), "it must not be denied that...".

Hannibalem: accusative subject belonging to the clause introduced by *tantō*, but placed before *tantō* for extra emphasis.

tantō...quantō: ablatives of degree of difference linking two correlative clauses with comparative sense (AG §414a), "by as much as (*quantō*)... by just as much (*tantō*)...". Nepos underscores the comparison between Hannibal and the Roman people by including the same five elements in each correlative clause.

Coordinator	Subject	Verb	Object	Virtue
tantō	*Hannibalem*	*praestitisse*	*cēterōs imperātōrēs*	*prūdentiā*
quantō	*populus Rōmānus*	*antecēdat*	*cūnctās nātiōnēs*	*fortitūdine*

prūdentiā...fortitūdine: ablatives of specification, like *virtūte* in the first sentence. Nepos contrasts the tactical brillance of Hannibal (*prūdentia*) and the resolute durability of the Romans (*fortitūdō*) that will enable the Romans to withstand Hannibal's initial victories, regroup, and ultimately prevail. Note how Nepos has framed the war as a contest between Hannibal and the Roman people rather than between Carthage and Rome, a theme he elaborates in the next paragraph.

antecēdat: subjunctive because it appears in a dependent clause in an indirect statement; it does not connote any sense of doubt or uncertainty (AG §591).

(2) Nam quotiēnscumque cum eō congressus est: note the frequent alliteration, a common feature of Nepos' style.

    eō: object of *cum*, referring to the masculine singular noun in the previous sentence (*populō Rōmānō*).

    congressus est: > *congredior*; Hannibal is the understood subject.

semper discessit superior: Nepos makes the same declaration about Hannibal's father, Hamilcar (who died in battle). Hannibal was repulsed from Nola three times (215–214 BC) and fought many indecisive battles in the last decade of the war. Nepos here follows the tenacious myth of Hannibal's invincibility in battle.

quod nisi: "but if (he had) not"; analogous to *quodsi*, "but if".

domī: locative (AG §428k), referring generally to Carthage and its politics, which was riven by long-running factional strife. One Carthaginian faction, represented by Hamilcar and his sons, favored an aggressive policy of expansion outside of Africa. They believed that cultivating trade and conquering new territory would make Carthage powerful enough to confront the existential threat posed by Rome. The other faction, led by Hanno the Great, favored the agricultural interests of Carthaginian landowners and further territorial expansion in Africa. Since Hanno's faction viewed Rome as just another regional power, they favored accommodation of Roman interests, provided Rome did not interfere in Carthage's African territory. As so often happens, these ideological differences became entangled with family vendettas and private grudges. Hanno, for example, sought to weaken the position of Hamilcar by publically accusing him of pederasty and of giving his daughter in marriage to his young lover, Hasdrubal the Fair, so that he could continue to enjoy Hasdrubal's affections. The limited support and reinforcements sent to Hannibal during his Italian campaign and Hannibal's dogged opposition to the landed aristocracy after the war should be viewed in the context of this long-running ideological and personal conflict.

vidētur: used personally with the infinitive, *potuisse*; "Hannibal seems likely to have been able...".

multōrum: subjective genitive (AG §343); i.e., many Carthaginians heaped abuse on Hannibal, rather than Hannibal reviled many people. Roman historians often framed their stories as a conflict between the genius and moral courage of a great individual and the envy and folly of the crowd. For more on the malice of the Carthaginian people towards Hannibal, see Livy 30.20.3–4.

(3) hic: i.e., Hannibal.

odium paternum: i.e., hatred possessed by his father (Hamilcar), not hatred of his father (by Hannibal). Nepos' use of *paternum* emphasizes that the *odium* of Rome is passed down (*relictum*) "like an inheritance" (*velut hērēditāte*) in Hannibal's family. In his *Life of Hamilcar*, Nepos states that this *odium* was the principal cause of the Second Punic War: "Hannibal, his son, was so led by his father's continual entreaties, that he would prefer to die than not make trial of the Romans" (4).

ergā: "towards, against" + accusative. Nepos, like Plautus and Tacitus, uses *ergā* with unfriendly feelings (*odium*); *ergā* is more typically used with expressions of friendly feelings, while the synonyms *contrā* and *adversus* are more common with unfriendly feelings.

sīc cōnservāvit, ut...dēposuerit: *sīc* signals a result clause, *ut...dēposuerit*, "he so *conservāvit* his *odium* that..." (AG §537). Result clauses are often signaled by words such as *tantus* (see 2.1, 5.2 below), *ita* (2.5), *adeō* (4.3), or *sīc* (12.3); but these markers are not required (10.6).

prius animam quam id dēposuerit: "he would sooner surrender his life than it" (*id*, i.e., *odium paternum*). Words implying comparison like *prius* are often followed by *quam* several words or even clauses later (AG §434) or they may be written as one word (e.g. *priusquam* in 7.6, 11.1). **dēposuerit:** perfect subjunctive in secondary sequence after *conservāvit*.

quī quidem: "because he, indeed"; *quī* introduces a relative clause of cause (AG §540c) with the subjunctive, *dēstiterit*.

cum: concessive cum clause (AG §549), "although..."

aliēnārum opum: "another's resources". After Hannibal was expelled from Carthage in 195 BC he assisted first King Antiochus III of Syria and then Prusias I of Bithynia in their wars against Rome, as Nepos goes on to explain.

animō: ablative of respect, "in his mind".

Chapter 2

Nepos flashes forward to Hannibal's arrival in the court of Antiochus the Great, after his exile from Carthage in 195 BC (1). Hannibal proves his loyalty to Antiochus by recounting how he swore an oath of eternal hatred against Rome before his father allowed him to join the army (2–5). Having finished the story of his oath, Hannibal exhorts Antiochus to spurn an alliance with Rome and to offer him command of Antiochus' forces (6).

(1) nam: this conjunction indicates that this sentence will justify or explain the last statement (AG §324h).

ut omittam: a common idiom, favored by Nepos' contemporary Cicero, "if I may pass over..." → "not to mention", "to say nothing of".

Philippum: King Philip V of Macedon (reigned 221–179 BC). After forging an alliance with Hannibal, Philip launched the First Macedonian War (214–205 BC). Hannibal, after his crushing victory at the Battle of Cannae (below, 4.4), enticed many cities of southern Italy and Sicily to revolt. Hannibal also received an embassy from Philip, who proposed an alliance against Rome. Although Philip possessed significant military resources, Rome's control of the sea prevented Philip and Hannibal from joining forces in Italy. After Philip had occupied large sections of Illyria in 212, the Romans attempted to neutralize Philip through diplomacy.

But after Philip defeated an anti–Macedonian coalition of Greek states and prevented a Roman expeditionary force from retaking Illyria, Rome negotiated a separate peace in 205. The treaty recognized Philip's territorial gains in Illyria, but Rome had won a more significant strategic victory by severing the alliance between Philip and Hannibal. And Rome had a long memory. Philip's reckoning would come almost a decade later when Rome crushed the Macedonians at the Battle of Cynocephalae in 197 BC, thus concluding the Second Macedonian War (200–197/6 BC). After the defeat, Philip was stripped of his independence, although he was allowed to remain on his throne.

absēns: refers to Hannibal; i.e., Hannibal sent an embassy that forged the anti–Roman alliance with Philip.

hostem: i.e., Philip, in apposition with the relative pronoun, *quem*.

Antiochus: King Antiochus III (the Great) of the Seleucid Kingdom (reigned 222–187 BC). Hannibal would flee to Antiochus' court in 195 BC (see 7.6–8.4).

hunc: Antiochus; Hannibal is the subject of *incendit*.

tantā cupiditāte: *tantā* signals the result clause, *ut...cōnātus sit inferre*.

bellandī: objective genitive, "for waging war" (AG §347); *bellandī* appears after the verb, *incendit*, for the sake of stylistic variety. Despite the tendency in Latin for the verb to come at the end of a sentence, authors routinely place a word or closely connected phrase after the verb to avoid monotony (AG §596a). Note that *Italiae* follows *cōnātus sit inferre* in the next clause. The same variation can be found in the next sentence with *Rōmānī, operam*, and *ad rēgem*.

ūsque ā rubrō marī: "all the way from the Red Sea". To the Romans, the *Mare Rubrum* (more frequently the *Mare Erythraeum*) referred to all of the waters around the Arabian Peninsula.

Italiae: dative with the compound verb, *inferre* (AG §370).

Roman legates attempt to undermine Hannibal's position in Antiochus' court.

(2) In this, the most complex sentence in the *Life*, Nepos first delineates the circumstances in which the main action occurs (clauses a–i) before at last revealing the main action (clause j).

(a) Ad quem cum lēgātī vēnissent Rōmānī,	circumstantial cum clause
(b) quī dē ēius voluntāte explōrārent	relative clause of purpose #1
(c) darentque operam,	relative clause of purpose #2
cōnsiliīs clandestīnīs,	ablative of means
(d) ut Hannibalem in suspīciōnem rēgī addūcerent,	substantive purpose clause explaining goal of action in (c)
(e) tamquam ab ipsīs corruptus alia atque anteā sentīret	clause of comparison explaining how (d) was accomplished
(f) neque id frūstrā fēcissent	circumstantial cum clause (a) resumes
(g) idque Hannibal comperisset	circumstantial cum clause continues
(h) sēque ab interiōribus cōnsiliīs sēgregārī vīdisset,	circumstantial cum clause continues
(i) tempore datō	ablative absolute or ablative of time
(j) adiit ad rēgem.	main clause

This sentence provides an excellent example of the Latin Period, the lengthy but logically coherent sentence structure that was favored by most Latin prose authors.

> (a) **Ad quem cum lēgātī vēnissent Rōmānī:** circumstantial *cum* clause describing an action that precedes the action of the main verb (AG §546). The *lēgātī Rōmānī*, led by Publius Villius Tappulus, arrived in Antiochus' court in 193/2 BC.
> **Ad quem:** i.e., King Antiochus. The connective relative links a sentence with an aspect of the preceding sentence (AG §308f). It is a device much favored by Nepos. Positioning a key word or phrase before the subordinating conjunction (*cum*) is very common in Latin.
> **vēnissent:** pluperfect subjunctive in secondary sequence indicating the action occurred before the perfect main verb *adiit*, likewise the verbs *fēcissent* (in clause f), *comperisset* (g), and *vīdisset* (h).

(b) **quī dē ēius voluntāte explōrārent:** relative clause of purpose expressing the reason that the *lēgātī vēnissent* (AG §531), "in order to gain information about his [i.e., Antiochus'] intentions". **explōrārent:** imperfect subjunctive in secondary sequence indicating that the action happened at the same time that the *lēgātī vēnissent Rōmānī*.

(c) **darentque operam...ut:** "and they endeavored to". The *–que* links the entire clause to the preceding thought.
cōnsiliīs clandestīnīs: ablative of means explaining how the *lēgātī darent operam*.

(d) **ut...addūcerent:** expresses the purpose towards which the *lēgātī Rōmānī* aimed when they *darent operam* (AG §563). **addūcerent:** frequently takes an accusative (*Hannibalem*) and a prepositional phrase denoting the place or state into which the accusative was led (*in suspīciōnem*).
rēgī: dative of reference denoting the person for whose benefit the action was accomplished, "in the eyes of the king" (AG §376).

(e) **tamquam ab ipsīs corruptus alia atque anteā sentīret:** the *Rōmānī lēgātī* pretend that Hannibal is *corruptus*.
tamquam: "as if...".
ab ipsīs: ablative of personal agent with *corruptus*; *ipsīs*, i.e., *lēgātīs Rōmānīs*.
alia atque anteā: idiomatic, "differently than before", object of *sentīret*, whose subject is Hannibal.

(f) **neque id frūstrā fēcissent:** the tense of *fēcissent* signals that the circumstantial *cum* clause has resumed. The circumstantial *cum* clauses continue in clause g (*comperisset*) and clause h (*vīdisset*).

(g) **comperi(vi)sset:** syncopated perfect (AG §181). Note the shift in number from plural to singular as Nepos moves to recounting Hannibal's actions.

(h) **ab interiōribus cōnsiliīs:** "more intimate councils", i.e., the King's inner circle of advisors.

(i) **tempore datō:** ablative absolute or ablative of time when, "when the opportunity presented itself" (to Hannibal).

(j) **adiit ad rēgem:** note how Nepos echoes the prefix of the verb (*ad–*) in the preposition (*ad*). Roman authors often favor wordplay that we avoid in formal writing (e.g. 2.4, 5.3, etc.).

10. Hannibal's Oath of Hatred Against Rome.
Drawing by Joelle Cicak, CC BY.

(3) eīque cum multa…commemorāsset: circumstantial *cum* clause (AG §546; as in 2.2 above). The subordinating conjunction (*cum*) is displaced from the start of its clause by a key word (the connective, *eī*). **eīque:** i.e., Antiochus; dative with *commemorā(vi)sset*, syncopated pluperfect subjunctive. **multa:** object of *commemorāsset*.

odiō: like *fidē*, an object of the preposition *dē*.

in Rōmānōs: "towards the Romans", "against the Romans".

puerulō mē: ablative absolute; since Latin lacks the present or perfect participle of *esse*, an ablative absolute can consist of a noun and adjective or two nouns in the ablative, as here (AG §419a; 7.2, 9.3, 12.2); **puerulō:** the diminutive of *puer* → "a little boy".

utpote nōn amplius novem annōs nātō: further specifies what Hannibal means by *puerulō mē*, i.e., when he was *nōn amplius novem annīs*. **nātō:** agrees with *mē*; "not being more than 9 years old", thus in 238/7 BC.

Karthāgine: locative, "in Carthage".

Iovī optimō maximō: "to Jupiter Optimus Maximus", the supreme Roman god. Nepos follows the Roman practice of using the name of the analogous Roman god in place of the Carthaginian deity, Baal.

(4) quae: connective relatives are often translated by "and" + the demonstrative, e.g., "and this...". Here, with *dum*, "and while this...."

vellemne: = *vellem–ne*, subjunctive in an indirect question introduced by *quaesīvit ā mē*.

in castra: metonymic for "on campaign".

id: i.e., the question that Hamilcar had asked (*vellemne sēcum in castra proficiscī*). **accēpissem:** as with English "accept", *accipiō* can denote the acceptance of a condition. **ab eō:** "from him" (Hamilcar), with *petere*.

nē dubitāret: negative substantive purpose clause dependent on *petere* (AG §563, sometimes called a jussive noun clause; 7.2, 8.1); *dubitō* + infinitive (*dūcere*; 11.3) often has the sense of "hesitate" (AG §558a n.2), "that he would not hesitate".

dūcere [mē]: *Remember that Hannibal is telling this anecdote.*

eam: the altar (*aram*); object of *tenentem*. It was customary to touch an altar when swearing an oath.

cēterīs remōtīs: ablative absolute; i.e., Hamilcar and Hannibal are alone.

numquam mē in amīcitiā cum Rōmānīs fore: an indirect statement indicating what Hannibal swore (*iūrāre*). **numquam:** placed first and separated from the verb *fore* for added emphasis.
  in amīcitiā: *amīcitia* in this context referred to a person or state that has placed itself in a subordinate but still independent relationship with Rome. Nepos' account of this episode is similar to that offered by Polybius ("never have good will towards the Romans", 3.11.7). Livy says that Hannibal instead swore "to be an enemy of the Roman people as soon as he was able" (21.1).
  fore: = *futūrum esse*.

(5) id ego: Latin authors like to juxtapose personal pronouns, even if doing so interrupts another phrase or clause (*id...iūs iūrandum*).

iūs iūrandum: a formal oath to complete a civil, military, or political obligation, sworn in the presence of a higher power—usually Jupiter or all the gods—but here to Hamilcar (*patrī datum*). Hannibal's *odium* is thus characterized not as a personal grudge but as a sacred (and public) obligation.

ūsque ad hanc aetātem: compare *ūsque ā rubrō marī* in 2.1.

ita cōnservāvī: *ita* signals the result clause, *ut...dēbeat*.

nēminī: dative of reference, "in the opinion of no one".

quīn...sim futūrus: "that I will be..."; *quīn* often introduces subjunctive clauses after negated expressions of hindering, resisting, and doubting (*nēminī dubium esse*, AG §558).

reliquō tempore: ablative of time, "for the rest (of my life)".

eādem mente: ablative of quality (AG §415), "of the same mind".

(6) Hannibal's speech concludes with a carefully structured sentence in which Hannibal warns Antiochus that the nature of their relationship rests on whether Antiochus intends to make peace with the Romans (*sī quid amīcē dē Rōmānīs cōgitābis*) or to wage war against them (*cum quidem bellum parābis*). To avoid confusion from the accumulation of conditionals, each half of the sentence is comprised of three parallel elements: 1) a general parameter (peace vs. war); 2) the result of Antiochus' action (act wisely vs. act foolishly); and 3) Antiochus' action (keep Hannibal in ignorance vs. not make him general).

sī quid: = *sī (ali)quid*: remember that after *sī, nisi, num*, and *nē* every *ali–* falls away.

amīcē: adverbial; i.e., if Antiochus entertains an alliance with Rome.

fēceris: future perfect tense, giving added emphasis to the future more vivid conditional, as do **cēlāris** and **posueris** (AG §516c).

nōn imprūdenter: "not unwisely". An example of litotes, in which an understatement or double negative implies the opposite → "very wisely".

mē cēlā(ve)ris: syncopated future perfect with an ablative of separation, "hide [it] from me".

quidem: introduces a clause that qualifies or opposes the preceding thought, "yet", "on the other hand".

in eō: "in this matter", referring to the action of the clause, *cum quidem bellum parābis*.

prīncipem: in apposition with *mē*, "me as leader".

Chapter 3

After his father's death Hannibal gains control of the army and campaigns in Spain (1–2). He crosses the Alps in November 218 BC and invades Italy (3–4).

(1) quā dīximus: "of which I spoke [above]" in 2.3. **quā:** the case of the relative pronoun is attracted to the case of its antecedent, *hāc...aetāte* (AG §306a); *quam dīximus* would be the more regular construction.

dīximus: ancient authors often referred to themselves using plural forms, especially in prose. Although the precise connotation of this common usage is debatable, it does not convey haughtiness or pretension, as the use of English "we" might in a similar circumstance (11.5).

cuius: i.e., Hamilcar; connective relative (AG §308f; see note on 2.4). Hamilcar was killed in 229 BC, either in battle by a flaming cart, or when he was ambushed while crossing a river.

Hasdrubale imperātōre suffectō: ablative absolute, "when Hasdrubal had been appointed replacement commander"; *suffectō* > *sufficiō*, the usual word for a person who substituted for a deceased or deposed magistrate, in this case referring to Hasdrubal "the Fair", brother–in–law of Hannibal and son–in–law of Hamilcar (not to be confused with Hasdrubal Barca, Hannibal's brother, who was defeated at the Battle of Metaurus in 207 BC).

praefuit: > *praesum* + dative, *equitātuī omnī*. Hannibal was 18 when he became leader of the Carthaginian calvary.

hōc quoque interfectō: ablative absolute. **hōc:** i.e., Hasdrubal the Fair. Hasdrubal was assassinated in 221 BC by a slave in revenge for his former master, whom Hasdrubal had killed.

exercitus: subject of *dētulit*.

summam imperiī: *summam* is feminine singular because it modifies an understood *rem*, "supreme command" (8.3).

ad eum: i.e., Hannibal.

id Karthāginem dēlātum: Hannibal's appointment to supreme command (*id*) was known by word of mouth (*dēlātum*) before it was confirmed officially.

Karthāginem: the accusative of "place towards which" does not require a preposition (AG §427.2).

dēlātum: "made known" (informally), in contrast to *relātum*, which would be used for official communications.

pūblicē: not "publicly" as opposed to "privately", but "officially" by the government in Carthage.

(2) minor quīnque et vīgintī annīs nātus: "born less than twenty–five years", i.e., "less than twenty–five years of age". Hannibal was actually 26 at the time. The use of *minor* + ablative with *nātus* to express age is atypical.

proximō trienniō: ablative of time within which, "in the course of the next three years". Although Nepos exaggerates the scope of Hannibal's exploits, he did conquer several independent tribes in the region.

bellō: ablative of means.

Saguntum, foederātam cīvitātem: located 90 miles south of the Iber River (modern Ebro), Saguntum was well within the sphere of Carthaginian influence according to the terms of the treaty that Hasdrubal signed with Rome in 226 BC. But since Saguntum had allied itself (*foederātam*) with Rome before Hasdrubal's treaty, Rome believed it remained her ally. Hannibal sacked Saguntum in 218 BC after an eight–month siege.

(3) ex hīs: i.e., *trēs exercitūs maximōs* in 3.2.

ūnum [exercitum] in Āfricam mīsit: this army was comprised of 13,850 infantry, 870 slingers, and 1,200 cavalry. Polybius claims to have seen a plaque erected by Hannibal that recorded the precise sizes of the three armies. Even so, ancient troop figures must be viewed with caution.

alterum cum Hasdrubale frātre in Hispāniā relīquit: this army of 12,600 infantry, 2,550 cavalry, and 21 elephants was to maintain Carthaginian control over its recent conquests in Hispania and resist the inevitable Roman counterattack.

tertium in Italiam sēcum dūxit: this army departed Carthago Nova in the late spring of 218 BC with as many as 90,000 infantry and 12,000 cavalry. It is doubtful that Hannibal planned to take such a large force into Italy. As many as 20,000 of the less experienced troops deserted or were released by Hannibal before the army arrived at the Rhône River. Hannibal stationed additional troops in garrisons to protect his lines of communication to Hispania. He arrived at the Alps with 38,000 infantry troops, 8,000 cavalrymen, and 37 war elephants.

saltum Pȳrēnaeum: in the singular, *saltum* refers to a mountain pass (compare the plural in 3.4 below).

quācumque: adverb, "in whichever way, wherever".

iter fēcit: slightly idiomatic, "he directed his course"; literally, "he made a journey". In Latin one may 'pave' (*sternit*), 'build' (**mūniit**, 3.4), or 'open' (**patefēcit**, 3.4) a road, but one may never 'make' (*facit*) one.

(4) Ad Alpēs posteāquam vēnit: temporal clause expanded by several subordinate clauses. The main clause begins with *Alpicōs cōnantēs*.

quae...sēiungunt, quās...trānsierat: two relative clauses whose antecedent is *Alpēs*.

ante eum: i.e., Hannibal. Nepos somewhat exaggerates Hannibal's accomplishment: the Gauls had migrated *en masse* into Italy over the Alpine frontier long before Hannibal. We might credit Hannibal as the first general to lead a "modern" army over the mountains against fierce local resistance. But Nepos is not splitting such hairs. Well before Nepos' time, the uniqueness of Hannibal's feat became an entrenched part of his legend. Nepos is simply following this tradition.

quō factō: ablative of cause, "in consequence of which".

saltus Grāius appellātur: Nepos relates the theory that this section of the Alps was called the *saltus Grāius* ("Greek pass") because the Greek Hercules (*Herculem Grāium*) had crossed though this area. During his Tenth Labor, Hercules drove the Cattle of Geryon (not an army as Nepos seems to imply) from the western island of Erytheia to King Eurystheus in Greece. Along the way, he supposedly fathered Galates, the ancestor of the Gauls. In fact, the name is almost certainly of native Celtic origin, meaning "precipitous" or "craggy". Such aetiologies, or stories of origins, were an important feature of the intellectual tradition in which Nepos wrote. It is not surprising that Nepos, who grew up in the shadow of the Alps, would include more detail about Hannibal's crossing. Local interest might motivate the added detail, but even here Nepos is distilling earlier accounts so as to focus on Hannibal's boldness and his leadership. Polybius boasts of having retraced the route himself (3.48.12) — as do many modern historians, if only by car.

trānsitū: ablative of separation with *prohibēre* (AG §401). We can either understand *transitū* with *prohibēre* ("to prevent the crossing") or with an implicit object, [*Hannibalem*] *prohibēre transitū*, "to prevent Hannibal from crossing".

concīdit: context requires that the verb be *concīdō, concīdere, concīdī, concisus* ("cut down, ruin, kill, destroy") rather than *concidō, concidere, concidī* ("fall down, die, perish"). Nepos is silent on the terrible losses inflicted on Hannibal's army by the mountain tribesmen and the frigid weather.

loca patefēcit, itinera mūniit, effēcit…rēpere: Note how Nepos has omitted conjunctions between these three coordinate clauses, a rhetorical device known as asyndeton (Greek for "unconnected"). Latin authors were especially fond of constructions in groups of three, also known as the tricolon. Compare the most famous asyndetic tricolon, Caesar's description of his victory at the Battle of Zela: *vēnī, vīdī, vīcī*.

> **itinera mūniit:** a technical phrase for the construction of roads. There were already routes through the Alps, although Hannibal did have to rebuild a section that had been destroyed by a landslide.
>
> **effēcit, ut…posset:** result clause.
>
> **eā [viā]:** serves as the antecedent for *quā*.
> **elephantus ōrnātus:** Hannibal's *elephantī* were *ornātī* in the sense that they were heavily-loaded with supplies, in contrast with the *homo inermis* who previously could not even crawl over the same ground.
> **rēpere:** "to crawl", contrasted with *īre*.

hāc: adverbial, "in this way".

Italiamque pervēnit: The raids by mountain tribes and the cold weather took a severe toll on Hannibal's army. The 900–mile march from Carthago Nova to Italy had taken 5 months. Crossing the Alps took 15 miserable days. Of the 38,000 infantry, 8,000 cavalry, and 37 war elephants that entered the Alps, no more than 20,000 infantry (12,000 Africans and 8,000 Spaniards), 6,000 cavalry, and only a few elephants reached Italy. The toll was horrific, but Hannibal's invasion of Italy thoroughly disrupted Rome's warplans. Rome would not regain the initiative until after seven savage years of fighting up and down the Italian peninsula. The planned invasion of Africa would be postponed by fourteen years. That is the measure of the strategic advantage that Hannibal had achieved by his unexpected invasion of Italy.

Chapter 4

Hannibal's stunning victories in Italy. He defeats the Romans at the Battle of Trebia in late December 218 BC (1–2). Disease costs him the use of his right eye, but he still manages to direct the ambush at Lake Trasimene in late June 217 BC (3). Hannibal annihilates two consular armies at the Battle of Cannae on 2 August 216 BC (4).

(1) cōnflīxerat and **pepulerat:** pluperfects expressing action completed before the crossing of the Alps in 3.4. Having told the story of Hannibal's march from Hispania to Italy in Chapter 3, this chapter will focus on his battles in Italy.

apud Rhodanum: "near the Rhône", a major river in southwest Gaul that flows into the Mediterranean near Marseilles. Not to be confused with the Island of Rhodes, *Rhodus –ī* f. Nepos exaggerates the scope of this battle, the first clash of the war between Roman and Carthaginian forces. It was, at most, a confused skirmish between small detachments of cavalry fought soon after Hannibal's forces crossed the Rhône, and before the arrival of Scipio's main force. After the skirmish, the bulk of Scipio's force continued towards Hispania; Hannibal moved north towards the Alps.

> **apud:** with a place name, *apud* always means "near"; it never means "in" (AG §428d).

cum P. Cornēliō Scīpiōne cōnsule: Publius Cornelius Scipio Asina was consul in 218 BC. He would die in Hispania in 211 BC while fighting Hannibal's brother, Hasdrubal. His son, Scipio Africanus, would defeat Hannibal at the decisive Battle of Zama in 202 BC.

hōc eōdem: i.e., Publius Cornelius Scipio Asina.

Clastidī: locative. Clastidium was a fortified town in Gallia Cispadana near the Po River (*apud Padum*). Captured from the Gauls in 222 BC, the town served as an important supply base for the Romans.

dēcernit: generally "to decide"; when applied to military affairs, *decernō* means "to decide by combat" and so, "to fight".

sauciumque inde ac fugātum: adjective and participle agreeing with implied *Scipionem*.

inde ac: "and then, and thereafter"; Nepos is careful to clarify that Scipio was wounded first and then retreated. Nepos' description is more appropriate for the Battle of Ticinus, a cavalry skirmish in late November or early December.

(2) tertiō: "for the third time"; Nepos refers to the Battle of Trebia, a small river that flows into the Po River near Genoa.

īdem Scīpiō: i.e., Publius Cornelius Scipio Asina; remember that *Scīpiō* is a third declension noun.

cum collēgā Tiberiō Longō: after Scipio was wounded at Ticinus, his co-consul Tiberius Sempronius Longus was recalled to confront Hannibal. He had recently taken Malta from the Carthaginians in preparation for the planned invasion of Africa.

adversus eum: preposition ("against") + accusative.

manum cōnseruit: a common idiom, "to join hand[s]" → "to join hand to hand (in battle)" → "to fight, join battle with", often with *cum* + ablative, *hīs* (i.e., Scipio and Longus).

per Ligurēs: the Ligurians lived in Gallia Cisalpina, near modern day Genoa. Roman authors often refer to a place by reference to its inhabitants.

Appennīnum: the Apennines are a major mountain range extending the length of peninsular Italy.

Etrūriam: Etruria is a region in north central Italy.

(3) hōc itinere: i.e., the march to Etruria (see 3.3).

adeō: signals the upcoming result clause, *ut...ūsus sit*.

gravī morbō: ablative of means. During his illness, Hannibal was carried on his one surviving elephant, a massive Indian elephant nicknamed Syrus or "The Syrian", which had a prosthetic metal tusk.

adficitur: historical present referring to a past action as though it is happening now. It was felt that this added vividness and excitement to the description (AG §469); Hannibal is the subject.

dextrō: ablative with the deponent verb, *ūsus sit* (AG §410).

86 Cornelius Nepos, *Life of Hannibal*

quā valētūdine: "by this affliction"; *valetūdō* can refer to good or bad health.
quā: connective relative (AG §308f; see above 2.4).

cum etiam tum premerētur lectīcāque ferrētur: concessive *cum* clause (AG §549), "although at the time...".

C. Flāminium...circumventum occīdit, neque multō post C. Centēnium... occupantem: Nepos deploys two parallel participial phrases to describe two Roman defeats. Each phrase is introduced by the name of a defeated Roman leader and concludes with a participle that agrees with the leader; other information about the battle is enclosed within the participle phrase.

C. Flāminium cōnsulem: after he was re-elected consul, Gaius Flaminius Nepos raised four new legions and marched north to meet Hannibal. As censor in 221/220 BC Flaminius oversaw the construction of the Circus Flaminius in Rome and the Via Flaminia, which connected Rome with Ariminum on the Adriatic coast.

Trasumēnum: Lake Trasimene, a large, picturesque lake in Umbria, about 85 miles north of Rome; according to Livy, it was "a place born for an ambush" (22.4.2).

circumventum: participle agreeing with *Flāminium*, not *Trasumēnum*.

neque multō post: adverbial, "not much after"; **multō**: ablative of degree of difference.

C. Centēnium: A few days after the Battle of Trasimene, Hannibal intercepted and annihilated a force of 4,000 elite cavalrymen (*cum dēlectā manū*) led by the propraetor Gaius Centennius.

saltūs: accusative plural object of *occupantem*; although in the singular, *saltus* refers to a narrow passage, in the plural it can refer to woods that contain clearings (compare 3.3).

(4) obviam: "towards, against, to meet" + dative, *eī*, with verbs of motion, *venērunt*.

duo cōnsulēs: Gaius Terentius Varro and Lucius Aemilius Paulus, allies of the Scipios, had campaigned for the consulship as staunch critics of Fabius Maximus' strategy of avoiding direct action against Hannibal (see 5.1). Despite his role in the defeat at Cannae, Varro continued to hold important military positions. Lucius Aemilius Paulus was killed at Cannae; his daughter, Aemilia Tertia, married Scipio Africanus.

utrīusque exercitūs: *exercitūs* is accusative plural, the object of *fugāvit*, "he routed", whose subject is Hannibal.

Cn. Servīlium Geminum: consul of 217 BC; after the disaster at Trasimene, Gnaeus Servilius Germinus led the fleet tasked with coastal defense of Italy and harassing raids against Carthaginian territory in north Africa.

superiōre annō: "in the previous year". The other consul from the previous year also fell in the battle. Again we find Nepos consciously avoiding a detailed account of military events. Even so, this is a surprisingly brief statement about the Battle of Cannae, the worst defeat suffered by Rome during the Second Punic War—and Hannibal's greatest triumph.

Essay on The Battle of Cannae & Its Legacy

> There was no longer any Roman camp, any general, any single soldier in existence.
> — Livy, *Ab urbe condita* 22.54

On August 2, 216 BC Rome suffered one of the most catastrophic defeats in military history. The town of Cannae, located about 300 miles south of Rome in Apulia, controlled the approaches to southern Italy and operated a granary important for supplying food to the city of Rome. There, on a flat, featureless plain, Hannibal accomplished a feat that was thought to be impossible: with his small army he enveloped a much larger Roman force. Surrounded and unable to maneuver, the Roman army disintegrated as a coherent fighting force.

According to Livy, 48,200 Romans were killed and another 20,000 captured before nightfall put a stop to the slaughter. Polybius puts the number of dead at 70,000. The victory had been costly for Hannibal as well. Nearly 6,000 of his troops fell in the battle. Modern historians tend to be more conservative about the size of the Roman army, but even so they put the number of Roman dead at around 30,000. Regardless of the exact toll, the greatest army that Rome had fielded to that point—a grand army assembled with the sole purpose of driving Hannibal out of Italy—had been annihilated. The consul Aemilius Paullus lay among the dead, as did both consular quaestors, 29 military tribunes, and another 80 men of senatorial rank. According to Livy, the surviving consul, Terentius Varro, escaped from Cannae with a mere fifty soldiers. The Roman defeat was total.

The scale of the slaughter at Cannae is difficult to comprehend. If the ancient estimates of casualties are accurate, Cannae saw the second deadliest single day of combat ever visited on a western army, and it is estimated that over one hundred Romans died every minute during the height of the battle. Regardless of the exact number of dead, there is no disputing the magnitude of the disaster that Hannibal had inflicted upon Rome, or the daring and brilliance he and his troops displayed on that day.

Hannibal's tactics at Cannae are often regarded as the most effective large-scale battle maneuvers in history, setting the standard by which military commanders continue to measure their success. Count Alfred von Schlieffen, the architect of Germany's strategy in World War I, believed that victory was possible for Germany provided that they followed Hannibal's example. As Dwight D. Eisenhower observed, "every ground commander seeks the battle of annihilation; so far as conditions permit, he tries to duplicate in modern war the classic example of Cannae".[2]

In the successive battles of Trebia, Trasimene, and Cannae, Hannibal had destroyed the equivalent of eight consular armies. In only 20 months he had killed as many as 150,000 men, or, by some estimates, one-fifth of all adult men in Rome and its allied cities. By way of comparison, that is three times the number of dead the (much more populous) United States lost in Vietnam, and thirty times the number lost in battle during the decade after 9/11. Even as Rome attempted to cope with these disasters, another befell them when the Gauls destroyed an army of 25,000 Romans near Litana in northern Italy.

In response to this unprecedented carnage, Rome's empire began to fracture. Capua, the second largest city in Italy, defected to Hannibal, as did several important cities in Apulia, Lucania, and Bruttium. Most troubling for the Romans, the 12 Latin cities, Rome's oldest and closest allies, declined to supply troops for the new army. Their mood was not placated when a proposal to enroll two senators from each Latin city into the depleted Senate was vehemently rejected (one senator even threatened to kill on sight any Latin who dared appear in the Senate). With Rome's alliances unraveling, Hannibal seemed poised for victory. At home, the treasury was bare and Rome resorted to loans to pay its troops. International opinion began to flow towards Hannibal and in 215 he signed an alliance with Philip V of Macedon. In Sicily, Hiero of Syracuse, a stalwart ally of Rome (and source of troops,

---

2   Eisenhower, D. 1948. *Crusade in Europe*, 325.

money, and grain) died and his grandson, Hieronymous, quickly shifted his support to Carthage.

Yet Rome still refused to surrender. The Romans appointed another dictator, Marcus Junius Pera, to organize the defense of Rome and begin levying new troops. Within a month of the disaster at Cannae, Rome could field four legions, even if these were composed of freed slaves and convicts. To divine the cause of the gods' displeasure they dispatched an envoy to consult the oracle at Delphi and to placate the gods they ordered the sacrifice of two Gauls and two Greeks. Hannibal, unable to besiege Rome because of his limited manpower and his need to provision his troops, bypassed the city and marched towards his new allies in Campania.

Hannibal's decision to bypass Rome after his victory at Cannae fostered one of the great military debates in antiquity. According to legend, after the battle the commander of Hannibal's cavalry suggested that Hannibal would be dining in victory on the Capitoline Hill within five days if he only had the courage to strike at the city. Centuries later, young Roman students were still assigned to debate his decision, as the Roman satirist Juvenal (ca. late first century AD) recalls:

> Every fifth day the teacher poisons me with his 'dreadful Hannibal'.
> The topic makes no difference: whether to attack Rome
> After Cannae, or after the downpour and lightening
> to lead away his troops, soaked by the storm.
> —Juvenal 7.160–164

Chapter 5

Hannibal outwits the dictator Fabius Maximus and escapes a blockade. These events happened before the Battle of Cannae (1). Hannibal's stratagem to break out of the blockade set by Fabius (2–4).

(1) hāc pugnā pugnātā: ablative absolute, as is *nullō resistente*. Intransitive verbs like *pugnō* can take a direct object when that object is a cognate noun, or a noun derived from the same linguistic root: e.g., *pugnāre pugnam* or *ludere ludum*.

Rōmam: accusative of motion towards, as is *Capuam* in the next sentence. Note that *profectus [est] > proficīscor* is an intransitive verb and so cannot take *Rōmam* as its object. In fact, Hannibal did not march on Rome until 211 BC.

in propinquīs urbī montibus: *montibus* is the object of the preposition, *in*; *urbī* is a dative with the adjective, *propinquīs*, "near the city".

aliquot (ibi) diēs: accusative of duration of time, "for some days (there)".

Q. Fabius Māximus: Quintus Fabius Maximus, who had twice been elected consul and had enjoyed a distinguished military career, was 58 years old when he was elected dictator in 217 BC.

dictātor Rōmānus: a dictator was elected to a six-month term to take decisive action during times of crisis. When the Senate determined that an imminent threat existed, a consul would announce during the dead of night that a dictator had been appointed (this had to take place in Rome). Although consuls and other magistrates remained in power during the dictator's term, the dictator exercised superior power, which included greater independence from the Senate, extensive power to punish without appeal, and immunity from prosecution for any decisions he made while in office.

in agrō Falernō: the *Ager Falernus* was a region north of Campania, best known for its outstanding "Falernian" wine.

eī: i.e., *Hannibālī*.

(2) hic: Nepos uses the demonstrative to indicate the change in subject back to Hannibal.

clausus: participle agreeing with *Hannibal*, the implicit subject of the sentence.

noctū: "by night, at night"; an archaic ablative form of *nox*.

exercitūs: genitive limiting *ullō dētrīmentō*.

imperātōrī: clarifies the ambiguous case of *Fabiō callidissimō*. Nepos also praises Hannibal as *callidus* (9.2; *De regibus* 3).

dedit verba: idiom, "he deceived". The implied contrast is with *facta* ("deeds"), an antithesis that is typical of Greek and especially Roman thought.

Hannibal's deception has nothing to do with *verba* or speech, showing how the idiom can be used in ways quite distinct from its literal meaning.

namque: the conjunction indicates that this sentence will justify or explain the preceding statement, as in 2.1 and 7.5.

obductā nocte: ablative of time when, "at nightfall"; literally, "with night having been drawn over (the sky)". The metaphor is not as strongly felt in Latin as it would be in English.

dēligāta: modifies *sarmenta*. Note how the participial phrase encloses *in cornibus iuvencōrum*, which explains where the *sarmenta* have been *dēligāta*.

ēiusque generis [iuvencōrum]: genitive limiting *multitudinem magnam dispālātam*, referring to the *iuvencī* with burning bundles of sticks between their horns (as opposed to another *genus iuvencōrum*).

dispālātam: > *dispālor*, "to wander around, straggle" (a very rare word). Hannibal had been victim of a similar strategy in 229 BC, when Iberian tribesman drove steer–drawn carts filled with flammable materials against the Carthaginian lines. According to Appian it was in this battle that his father Hamilcar was killed by a flaming ox–cart (others say he drowned).

quō: connective relative agreeing with *vīsū*.

repentīnō: adverb; *repente* is the more common form, but *repentīnō* is not uncommon in Livy, Caesar, Cicero, and Apuleius.

vīsū: noun in an ablative absolute with the participle *obiectō*. The participle helps distinguish the noun from the identical form of the supine (AG §508–510; e.g., *Aeneid* 12.252: *mīrābile vīsū*, "amazing to behold"). The supine is never modified by an adjective or participle.

tantum terrōrem: *tantum* signals the result clause, *ut...sit ausus*.

iniēcit: the subject is Hannibal.

exercituī: dative with a compound verb, *in–iēcit* (AG §370).

(3) hanc post rem gestam: the demonstrative *hanc* refers back to Hannibal's stratagem in the previous sentence. Nepos has placed *hanc* before its preposition to underscore the connective nature of the demonstrative.

Authors also regularly place an element of a prepositional phrase (usually an adjective) before the preposition for balance, as in *magnā cum laude*.

post...nōn ita multīs diēbus: ablative of time when, "not so many days after".

M. Minucium Rūfum, magistrum equitum: the "Master of the Cavalry" served as the dictator's deputy and was usually appointed by the dictator. But because the surviving consul could not reach Rome after Trasimene, Rufus was elected at the same time as Fabius Maximus.

    equitum: genitive plural, "of the horsemen" → "of the Cavalry".

parī ac dictātōrem imperiō: "with an authority equal to that of the dictator". The creation of, in effect, a co–dictator was unprecedented and indicates the desparate circumstances in which the Romans found themselves.

    dictātōrem: accusative under the influence of the accusative *magistrum*. Strictly speaking a dative, *dictātōrī*, might be expected with *parī*. But since the phrase *parī ac dictātōrī imperiō* would be confusing, Nepos places *dictātōrem* in the accusative, indicating that Rufus was Magister Equitum and, in essence, dictator with power equal to that held by Fabius.

    parī imperiō: ablative of quality (AG §415). *Imperium* refers to the authority to command in military and judicial contexts (3.1, 7.3).

prōductum: participle agreeing with *Rufum*, "(having been) led into, lured".

Ti. Semprōnium Gracchum: Tiberius Sempronius Gracchus, consul in 216 BC, proconsul in 214, and reelected consul in 213 (*iterum cōnsulem*); great–uncle of the famous reformers Tiberius and Gaius Gracchus.

    Gracchum, iterum cōnsulem...Marcellum, quīnquiēns cōnsulem: Nepos confuses who was in office in 212 BC. Gracchus was consul in 213 and died in 212, after his consulship. The correct usages would be *bis consulem* and *quintum consulem*. Confusion about the how to count consulships, however, was so common that Aulus Gellius catalogued notable mistakes in a short essay, which included some humorous advice by Cicero to Pompey. When Pompey was unsure whether he should inscribe *tertium* or *tertio* on the dedication of his theater in Rome, Cicero advised he should just avoid the question by using the abbreviation "TERT".

in Lūcānīs: "among the Lucanians", a tribe who lived in southern Italy. This phrase continues the sequence of information about Gracchus: 1) *iterum cōnsulem*, 2) *in Lūcānīs*, and 3) *in īnsidiās inductum*.

absēns: i.e., Hannibal, who was away from the army when the battle was fought.

in īnsidiās inductum: Gracchus was said to have been ambushed and killed while bathing with a small group of men as his army marched to support the siege of Capua.

M. Claudium Marcellum: Marcus Claudius Marcellus (ca. 268–208 BC) was among the most illustrious Romans during this period. Marcellus was one of only three Roman generals to have won the *spolia opima* ("rich spoils"), when he killed the Gallic king Viridomarus in single combat at the First Battle of Clastidium in 222 BC. Winning the *spolia opima*, awarded to a Roman general who stripped the armor of an enemy leader after killing him in single combat, was the highest honor a Roman could achieve. Earlier in the Second Punic War, Marcellus had twice repulsed Hannibal from the strategic city of Nola. He had captured the major Sicilian city of Syracuse after a protracted siege, during which the scholar and inventor Archimedes was killed. For the losses he inflicted on the enemies of Rome, Marcellus earned the nickname, "the Sword"—recall that Fabius Maximus was called "the Shield".

apud Venusiam: a town in Apulia near Mount Vultur. It is best known as the birthplace of the poet Horace (65–8 BC).

parī modō: i.e., *in īnsidiās indictum*. Marcellus was ambushed while on a reconnaissance mission with a small band of cavalry. The ambushes of Gracchus and Marcellus are typical of the indecisive victories won by Hannibal during the later stages of the war in Italy.

(4) longum: neuter with infinitive, *ēnumerāre*; "it would be (too) long", in the sense of "tedious". English idiom requires the subjunctive ("would"); in Latin, the indicative is used.

ex quō intellegī possit: relative clause of result (AG §537.2); the subject of *possit* is provided by the indirect question, *quantus ille fuerit*.

quantus: interrogative adjective introducing an indirect question with the subjunctive, *fuerit*.

eī: dative with the compound verb, *re–stitit*.

in aciē: "in battle" (see also 6.4, 11.1).

adversus eum: the first of three consecutive prepositional phrases (*post Cannēnsem pugnam; in campō*). Latin authors usually avoided stringing together prepositional phrases in this way.

Cannēnsem: adjective modifying *pugnam*.

in campō: "in the open field, on open ground". This is an exaggeration, but one made by many historians, even to this day. In fact Roman and Carthaginian forces were constantly skirmishing and they engaged in over a dozen significant battles in Italy after Cannae (see the "Chronology of Hannibal's Life"). After Cannae, however, no Roman army in Italy dared challenge Hannibal on level ground, where Hannibal's cavalry could provide a decisive advantage.

The End of Hannibal's Campaign in Italy (218–203 BC)

After Hannibal's wild success in the first years of the war, the Romans avoided set battles on terrain where Hannibal's superior cavalry could produce the kind of devastating losses that were seen at Trebia and Cannae. Fabius' strategy of harassment and delay would prove sound. By avoiding a disastrous defeat that would provoke further defections to Hannibal, Rome gained the time to wear down Hannibal's army and retake rebel cities throughout Samnium and Liguria.

By 211 BC, Rome was able to field 25 legions while its fleet raided Africa. In the same year Rome recaptured Syracuse and Capua, depriving Hannibal of vital bases of operations and destroying his credibility as a reliable ally against Roman aggression. Rome executed the leaders of Capua and sold many Capuan men, women, and children into slavery; those who survived were stripped of their citizenship and sent into exile. The example had been made: no further cities defected to Hannibal's side.

Hannibal and his lieutenants were still capable of overpowering small forces of Romans, ravishing the Italian countryside, capturing the occasional city, and inflicting the rare larger defeat, as when Roman armies were destroyed at Herdonea in 212 BC and again in 210. For the most part, however, the Romans did avoid set battles and Hannibal was thus denied a decisive victory that would compel the Romans to sue for peace. Hannibal's strategic situation continued to darken during the next few years: Fabius retook the vital port of Tarentum in 209 BC; Sicily was pacified; and any hope of reinforcement from Philip in Greece was lost. Hannibal was increasing penned in the south of Italy.

In 207 BC, Hannibal attempted to regain the initiative. He summoned his brother Hasdrubal from Spain with a large army. Rome was forced to react to prevent the nightmare of a massive combined army in Italy under the command of the sons of Hamilcar. In a reverse of Hannibal's successes early in the war, the consular armies of Marcus Livius and Gaius Claudius Nero (ancestor of the famous emperor) outmaneuvered and annihilated Hasdrubal's exhausted army at the Metaurus River. Hannibal only learned of the disaster when the severed head of his brother was tossed into his camp.

Unable to sustain offensive operations in central Italy, Hannibal retreated to the region of Bruttium, in the toe of Italy's boot. Although Hannibal and his lieutenants continued to raid throughout Italy, the tide had turned. Scipio's victory at Ilipa the following year (206 BC) removed any chance of reinforcement from Spain. Hannibal would remain isolated in southern Italy for two more years as the Romans debated their next move. When Scipio at last invaded Africa in 204 BC, Hannibal was forced in the autumn of 203 BC to return and defend a homeland that he had left 35 years before. His great gamble had failed. The war would be settled not on the fields of Italy but outside the walls of Carthage.

Chapter 6

Hannibal, although still unbeaten in Italy, is recalled to Africa (1–2). He is defeated by Scipio at the Battle of Zama, October 202 BC (3). He avoids a Numidian ambush and raises a new army in Hadrumetum (4).

(1) hinc: "next" (as in 4.3).

dēfēnsum: supine, used to express purpose after a verb of motion, *revocātus* (AG §509). As a verbal noun the supine can take a direct object, *patriam*.

P. Scīpiōnem, fīlium ēius: Publius Cornelius Scipio (236–183 BC), son of Publius Cornelius Scipio Asina (4.1–2). Scipio ranks as one of Rome's greatest generals. After he completed the Roman conquest of Hispania (210–206 BC) he was elected consul at the age of only 31, with the assumption that he would lead the invasion of Africa. But Fabius Maximus and other conservative leaders in the Roman Senate feared the continued presence of Hannibal in southern Italy and the audacity of the young Scipio. Assigned to Sicily without an army, he raised a volunteer force of cavalry and eventually won permission to invade Africa. In 203 BC he destroyed an army of Carthaginian and Numidian forces near Utica by burning down their camp. Scipio's defeat of Hannibal at Zama in the following year would earn him the agnomen, "Africanus".

prīmō apud Rhodanum, iterum apud Padum, tertiō apud Trebiam: Hannibal's series of victories over Scipio Asina (4.1).

fugā(ve)rat: syncopated perfect (AG §181), "he had put to flight". Note the difference between transitive verb, *fugō, fugāre* ("to put to flight"), and the intransitive verb, *fugiō, fugere* ("to flee").

(2) cum hōc: i.e., Publius Scipio (the future Africanus). Observe how Nepos' desire to open the sentence with a connective demonstrative (*hōc*) results in the positioning of the prepositional phrase before the ablative absolute.

exhaustīs iam patriae facultātibus: ablative absolute, with causal sense. **iam:** emphasizes a moment in time that contributes to the state of affairs that is being described, "at this point" rather than "now" or "then".

inpraesentiārum: adverb, "at present, under the present circumstances"; a colloquial contraction of the phrase, *in praesentiā rērum*.

bellum compōnere: an idiom, "to make a temporary truce"; compare *foedus*, a permanent treaty (*foederātam cīvitātem*, 3.2; *ex foedere*, 7.5). The intense alliteration (*compōnere...congrederētur. In colloquium convēnit; condiciōnēs nōn convēnērunt*) has the effect of rendering the meeting between Scipio and Hannibal as the climax of the war, after which Hannibal's shocking defeat is an anticlimax.

quō: introduces a relative clause of purpose with the subjunctive, *congrederētur*, expressing why Hannibal desired to *bellum compōnere* (AG §531).

condiciōnēs nōn convēnērunt: *condiciōnēs* must be the subject of the intransitive *convēnērunt*, "terms (of peace) were not agreed upon".

(3) paucīs diēbus: "within a few days" (6.4, 10.4). The battle actually took place the day after the conference.

apud Zamam: The exact site of the battle is unknown, but it likely took place between Sicca Veneria and Zama Regia, approximately 75 miles southwest of the city of Carthage. At Zama Hannibal was at last able to deploy war elephants against the Romans, but to little effect, since Scipio had developed tactics to minimize their effectiveness and Hannibal was forced to use young, untrained elephants that took fright and trampled the Carthaginian lines. Scipio triumphed when his superior Numidian cavalry routed its Carthaginian counterpart and attacked the Carthaginian rear lines. While Roman losses in the battle numbered under 2,000, nearly ten times as many Carthaginians died.

cum eōdem: i.e., Publius Scipio.

incrēdibile dictū: the ablative supine, *dictū*, is used to indicate an action in reference to an adjective, *incrēdibile*: "unbelievable to say". Nepos expresses his amazement because this is the first time that Hannibal is defeated in battle (5.4) and because he was able to march a defeated army a great distance across difficult ground in only two days.

bīduō et duābus noctibus: ablative of time when. The march was uninterrupted, continuing day and night.

Hadrūmētum: accusative of place towards which, with *pervēnit*.

mīlia passuum trecenta: genitive of the whole (AG §346), "300,000 paces" or 300 Roman miles. The actual distance from Zama to Hadrumetum is closer to 100 Roman miles. Nepos may exaggerate the distance to render Hannibal's achievement that much more impressive, or he may be following a mistaken source.

(4) Numidae: the Numidians lived in the Carthaginian hinterlands and were known for their expert cavalry. The defection of the Numidians to Scipio was a significant blow to Carthaginian military power.

eī: dative with *insidiātī sunt*.

nōn sōlum...sed etiam: a common parallel construction, "not only...but also..." (7.5).

98   Cornelius Nepos, Life of Hannibal

reliquōs ē fugā: i.e., the troops who survived the rapid retreat from Zama.

Hadrūmētī: locative.

novīs dīlēctibus: "by new levies". Note that even as Carthage sues for peace, Hannibal prepares to fight on; compare how Nepos framed the war as a contest between Hannibal and the Roman people rather than between Carthage and Rome (1.1–1.2).

Chapter 7

Peace between Rome and Carthage. For a time Hannibal continues to fight, but then is elected to political office (1–4). Carthage begins a rapid recovery after Hannibal institutes a series of political and economic reforms (5). Hannibal is forced into exile (6). Carthage fails to arrest Hannibal. He is declared an outlaw (7).

(1) in apparandō [bellum]: gerund (AG §502), "in preparing [war]".

ācerrimē occupātus: "most actively engaged". Note how Nepos maintains the distinction between Hannibal and the Carthaginians.

bellum...composuērunt: an idiom, "to make a temporary truce" (see 6.4). The terms of the peace treaty were harsh. Carthage agreed to abandon all claims to territory outside of Africa, to pay a yearly indemnity of 200 talents for 50 years (a total of almost 260 tons of silver), to reduce its navy to ten warships (Scipio burned over 500 ships outside of Carthage's harbor in a spectacular demonstration of Rome's victory), and never to make war without Rome's permission. It was the violation of this last term, under duress, that precipitated the Third Punic War (149–146 BC) and the destruction of Carthage.

Ille: i.e., Hannibal, subject of *praefuit* and *gessit*.

sētius: comparative of *secus*, "otherwise, differently"; usually with a negative (*nihilō*): "not at all differently" → "as if nothing happened". Hannibal retained command of the Carthaginian army, which continued to support him. Perhaps Carthage feared a reprise of the devastating "Mercenary War" if they moved against Hannibal.

nihilō: ablative of degree of difference.

praefuit: > *praesum* + dative, *exercituī*.

rēsque in Āfricā gessit: i.e., *in Āfricā pugnāvit* (8.4).

ūsque ad P. Sulpicium C. Aurēlium cōnsulēs: "even until the consulship of..."; i.e., in 200 BC. Rome subsequently demanded that Carthage recall all military commanders from Italy and adhere to the terms of the peace treaty. Publius Sulpicius Galba Maximus was consul in 211 BC, when he defended Rome from a surprise attack by Hannibal. He led the first Roman fleet into the Aegean and captured Aegina in 210 BC. Dictator in 203, he was the last Roman to hold this position until Sulla in 82/81 BC. In 200, he commanded Roman forces in the Second Macedonian War. Gaius Aurelius Cotta was sent to reinforce the garrison at Ariminium after several Gallic tribes allied with Carthage sacked the town of Placentia in northern Italy and threatened Cremona.

(2) This complex sentence is manageable if read in sequence with careful attention to the parallel sequence of its clauses. Nepos begins with an ablative absolute that conveys the context (a) in which the main action occurs (b). He then explains why the Carthaginians undertook that action (c–h).

(a) hīs enim magistrātibus,	ablative absolute
(b) lēgātī Karthāginiēnsēs Rōmam vēnērunt	main clause
(c) quī senātuī populōque Rōmānō grātiās agerent,	relative clause of purpose #1
(d) quod cum iīs pācem fēcissent,	causal clause
(e) ob eamque rem corōnā aureā eōs dōnārent,	relative clause of purpose #2
(f) simulque peterent	relative clause of purpose #3
(g) ut obsidēs eōrum Fregelliīs essent	substantive purpose clause #1
(h) captīvīque redderentur.	substantive purpose clause #2

Nepos, as he did in the long sentence in 2.2, uses the enclitic *–que* to signal the connections between parallel elements: *–que* in (e) and (f) link those clauses to the series of relative clauses of purpose that begins in (c); the *–que* in (h) links the two substantive purpose clauses in (g) and (h) that are introduced by *peterent* in (f).

(a) hīs enim magistrātibus: ablative absolute, referring to the consuls of 200 BC mentioned in 6.1. Since Latin lacks the present or perfect participle of *esse*, an ablative absolute can consist of a noun and adjective or two nouns in the ablative, as here (AG §419a; similar constructions can be found in 2.3, 9.3, and 12.2).

(b) Rōmam: accusative of place towards which.

(c) quī senātuī populōque Rōmānō grātiās agerent: relative clause of purpose with a subjunctive, *agerent*, expressing the reason why the *lēgātī Karthāginiēnsēs Rōmam vēnērunt* (AG §531).

> **senātuī populōque Rōmānō:** datives with the idiom, *grātiās agerent*, "gave thanks". Nepos' use of *senātus populusque Rōmānus* is anachronistic, since the Romans only began to use the phrase to refer to their state in the early first century BC.

(d) quod cum iīs pācem fēcissent: causal *quod* clause (AG §540).

cum iīs: i.e., the Carthaginians.

> **fēcissent:** pluperfect subjunctive after *quod*, because it is part of what the Carthaginian delegates said to the Romans (i.e., "O Romans, we thank you for having made peace").

(e) ob eamque rem corōnā aureā eōs dōnārent: relative clause of purpose with a subjunctive, *dōnārent*. Because *ob eamque rem* is equivalent to *quam ob rem*, the phrase can introduce a relative clause of purpose despite the absence of an explicit relative pronoun.

> **ob eamque rem:** preposition + accusatives, referring to the making of peace in the preceding clause; *-que* links the entire clause to the relative clause of purpose (c).
>
> **eōs:** i.e., the Romans.
>
> **dōnārent:** governing the accusative, *eōs*, + ablative of item given, *corōnā aureā*.

(f) simulque peterent: relative clause of purpose with a subjunctive, introducing a clause that indicates what the *lēgātī Karthāginiēnsēs peterent*.

(g) ut obsidēs eōrum Fregellīs essent: substantive purpose clause (AG §563, sometimes called a jussive noun clause), dependent on *peterent*.

> **eōrum:** i.e., the Carthaginians; the reflexive pronoun *suī* would be more regular. Those signing a treaty often sent or exchanged hostages, whose lives would be forfeit if the treaty were broken.
>
> **Fregellīs:** locative; the town of Fregellae, about halfway between Rome and Capua on the Via Latina, remained loyal to Rome during the Second Punic War.

(h) captīvīque redderentur: another substantive purpose clause, dependent on *peterent*. **captīvī:** Carthaginians captured during the Second Punic War.

(3) hīs: i.e., *lēgātī Karthāginiēnsēs*.

respōnsum est: impersonal (note the neuter ending), "this was the response"; it introduces three indirect statements:
  a) *mūnus + acceptumque esse*
  b) *obsidēs + futūrōs [esse]*
  c) *captīvōs + remissūrōs [esse]*

quō locō rogārent and **cuius operā susceptum bellum foret** and **quod Hannibalem...habērent:** subjunctives because they appear in subordinate clauses in indirect discourse (AG §580); *rogārent* and *haberent* are imperfect, indicating action contemporary with the past tense main verb, *respōnsum est* (AG §483); *susceptum foret* (= *susceptum esset*) is pluperfect, indicating action prior to the main verb.

quō locō: ablative of place.

quod Hannibalem...habērent: explains why the Romans will not release their prisoners of war (*captīvōs*).
  Hannibalem: object of *habērent*, whose plural subject must be *Karthāginiēnsēs*.
  cuius operā: "by whose efforts"; the Carthaginians had been attempting to disassociate themselves from Hannibal but the Romans remind them that they share responsibility for his actions.
  inimīcissimum nōminī Rōmānō: *inimīcus* is used to describe someone with an active hatred of someone or something, "full of hate, hateful, hostile, unfriendly" (+ dative), rather than "hated"; therefore *inimīcissimum* must modify *Hannibalem*, rather than *bellum*. **nōminī Rōmānō:** "to whatever is called Roman", i.e., Roman dominion, nation, power.

itemque: "likewise, further"; *itemque introduces an additional point of information.*

(4) hōc respōnsō Karthāginiēnsēs cognitō: ablative absolute. *Karthāginiēnsēs*, the subject of *revocārunt*, is positioned within the ablative absolute to signal that it was the Carthaginians who understood the response of the Roman delegation.

revocā(vē)runt: syncopated perfect (AG §181).

domum: accusative of place to which, without a preposition (AG §427).

ut rediit: *ut* + indicative is strictly temporal, "when".

rēx: the Carthaginian title was *suffes*, or "judge". Two *suffetes* were elected annually to serve as the chief civilian officers of the Carthaginian government. They were akin to the Roman consuls, as Nepos explains in the next sentence. Hannibal was elected to this office in 196 BC.

annō secundō et vīcēsimō: ablative of time when. Hannibal had been general for 22 years.

ut enim Rōmae cōnsulēs, sīc Karthāgine: *ut...sīc*: correlatives, "(just) as... so..." (AG §323g). *Rōmae* and *Karthāgine* are locative.

quotannīs: adverb, "every year".

annuī: "annual", i.e., "for the duration of one year".

bīnī rēgēs: "two kings at a time, a pair of kings".

creābantur: *creō, -āre* is the technical term for electing public officials.

(5) parī...ac: adjectives and adverbs of likeness (such as *parī*) are often followed by *ac*, "as, just so" (AG §384 n. 2).

parī dīligentiā: ablative of quality (AG §415).

namque: the conjunction indicates that this sentence will justify or explain the preceding statement.

ex novīs vectīgālibus: ablative of source (AG §403). Nepos uses a common stylistic device of having the preposition (*ex*) repeat the prefix of the verb (*ef–fēcit > ec > ex*). Hannibal in fact avoided the imposition of new taxes by reducing waste and embezzlement. Understand as "by means of a reformed [system of] taxation".

nōn sōlum ut esset pecūnia...sed etiam superesset: correlatives, "not only...but also..." (6.4), establishing the parallel between the two result clauses with the subjunctive.

quae Rōmānīs ex foedere penderētur: relative clause of purpose (AG §540c); its antecedent is *pecūnia*. **ex foedere:** "in accordance with the treaty".

superesset: "there would remain" → "there would be a surplus (of money)"; the subject is *pecūnia*.

quae in aerāriō repōnerētur: relative clause of purpose (AG §540c).

(6) M. Claudiō L. Fūriō cōnsulibus: i.e., in 196 BC.

Rōmā: ablative of place from which (AG §427.1).

Karthāginem: accusative of place towards which (3.1).

hōs: i.e., *legātōs Rōmānōs*; note how the demonstrative appears first in the sentence, signaling how this sentence relates to the last.

ratus: > *reor*; the perfect participles of many deponent verbs are equivalent to English present active participles: "suspecting that...".

suī exposcendī grātiā: *grātiā* ("for the sake of") with a preceding genitive, *suī exposcendī* (AG §504b); *exposcendī* is a gerundive agreeing with the reflexive personal pronoun *suī*. When the gerund appears in a construction in which it would take an accusative—e.g. *sē exposcendī grātiā*, "for the sake of demanding him (Hannibal)"—Roman authors preferred using a gerundive (AG §503). Hoping to engineer Hannibal's ouster, Hannibal's domestic enemies had appealed to Rome indicating that the general had forged a secret alliance with Antiochus III. In Rome, Scipio Africanus deemed it beneath the dignity of the Roman people to entertain the scurrilous attack. His advice was not heeded and Rome began to move against Hannibal.

missōs [esse]: perfect passive participle agreeing with *hōs* in an indirect statement dependent on *ratus*.

priusquam iīs senātus darētur: *darētur* is subjunctive because it contains a logical connection to the main action of the sentence, *nāvem ascendit* (11.1).
    senātus darētur: *senātus dare* is an idiom, "to give an audience to" + dative (*iīs*); *senātus*: the Carthaginian council of 300 aristocrats; Nepos continues to use Roman terms to describe Carthaginian institutions.

ad Antiochum: masculine, therefore King Antiochus III of the Seleucid Kingdom (see note on 2.1) not the city of Antioch, *Antiochia, –ae* f.

(7) hāc rē palam factā: ablative absolute, "when this (Hannibal's flight) became known". Hannibal first fled to his personal fortress to the south of Carthage. He then sailed to the nearby Cercina Islands. There, he narrowly evaded arrest by the sailors of a Carthaginian ship by claiming he was on a diplomatic mission to Tyre. Hannibal invited the sailors to a banquet, requesting that they bring their sails as awnings against the scorching sun. While the sailors slept, Hannibal stole their sails and weighed anchor, sailing to Tyre, and from there to the court of Antiochus.

Poenī: i.e., *Karthāginiēnsēs*.

quae eum comprehenderent: relative clause of purpose expressing why the *Poenī nāvēs mīsērunt* (AG §531).

sī possent cōnsequī: Nepos wrote the subjunctive *possent* because its clause represents an action that is integral to the subjunctive clause on which it depends: the ships could not arrest Hannibal if they did not catch him first (AG §593).

bona ēius pūblicā(vē)runt: syncopated perfect (AG §181), as is *iūdicā(vē)runt*. **bona:** in the plural, *bonus* can refer to "property", as in the English "goods".

domum ā fundāmentīs disiēcērunt: a common penalty inflicted on exiles, fallen tyrants, and other public enemies in antiquity. Clodius razed Cicero's house when he was exiled in 58 BC.

Chapter 8

Hannibal renews his attempts to rally Carthage against Rome (1). The Death of Mago (2). Nepos condemns Antiochus for ignoring Hannibal's advice (3). The navy of Rhodes defeats Hannibal at the Battle of Eurymedon, 190 BC (4).

(1) L. Cornēliō Q. Minuciō cōnsulibus: i.e., in 193 BC; Lucius Cornelius Merula and Quintus Minucius Thermus were fighting Gallic tribes in northern Italy.

in fīnibus Cȳrēnaeōrum: Cyrene was a province of Ptolemaic Egypt, to the east of Carthage's territory in North Africa.

spē fīdūciāque: ablatives of cause, "because of their hope and confidence in Antiochus" (*Antiochī*, objective genitive).

cui iam persuāserat: the antecedent of *cui* is *Antiochī*; Nepos told the story of how Hannibal convinced Antiochus to attack the Romans in 2.1–2.3. Hannibal did not, however, succeed in convincing the king to send an army to Italy.

ut...proficīscerētur: substantive purpose clause (AG §563), with Antiochus as its subject; the sudden switching of subjects within a complex sentence is typical of Latin. Here, since Hannibal must persuade someone else (i.e., Antiochus), the new subject is understood.

hūc: i.e., *in finibus Cȳrēnaeōrum*.

(2) Magōnem eādem, quā frātrem, absentem affēcērunt poenā: note the separation of nouns from their adjectives, *eādem...poenā* and *Magōnem...absentem*.

poenā: ablative of price, which is used to indicate an indefinite penalty or the exact amount of a fine (AG §416).

illī: i.e., Hannibal and Mago.

dēspērātīs rēbus: ablative absolute, with causal sense.

cum solvissent nāvēs ac vēla ventīs dedissent: circumstantial *cum* clause describing actions that precede the action of the main verb, *pervēnit* (AG §546). **solvissent nāvēs:** "release the ships" → "weigh anchor". This sentence provides a good illustration of the factors that a Roman author weighed when determining the order of words in a sentence. The subordinating conjunction *cum* would naturally come at the start of the sentence. But because the action of the ablative absolute, *dēspērātīs rēbus*, must precede that of the *cum* clause—the situation must be hopeless before Hannibal and Mago decide to flee—Nepos places the ablative absolute before *cum*. Because Nepos likes to begin sentences with connectives and demonstratives, *illī*, although it is part of the *cum* clause, appears first, followed by the ablative absolute, and then the rest of the *cum* clause.

duplex memoria: "double memory"; i.e., there were two accounts of Mago's death.

aliī...aliī: a correlative construction, "some...others...".

ā servulīs: ablative of personal agent. Other sources indicate that Mago was wounded while fighting the Romans in Cisalpine Gaul and died of his wounds en route to Carthage in 203 BC.

scrīptum relīquērunt: literally, "leave behind a written record"—compare the English expression "leave a paper trail"—a common periphrasis equivalent to *scrīpsērunt* (13.1), introducing an indirect statement with *eum* as its accusative subject and the infinitive, *interfectum* [*esse*].

(3) sī tam...pārēre voluisset, quam...īnstituerat: *tam* and *quam* are correlatives (AG §323; 9.4) in the protasis of a past contrary to fact conditional.

in agendō bellō: gerundive, see note on 7.6.

pārēre: takes the dative, *cōnsiliīs*.

voluisset: subjunctive in the protasis of a past contrary to fact conditional, "if he had been willing (but he was not)" (9.1).

in suscipiendō [bellō]: gerundive, parallel with *in agendō bellō*.

propius Tiberī quam Thermopylīs: *propius* can be taken with the dative (*Tiberī, Thermopylīs*), although the accusative is more common. Antiochus was defeated by the Romans at Thermopylae in 191 BC and compelled to withdraw to Asia.

dē summā [rē] imperiī: "about supreme command" (3.1).

quem: connective relative; its antecedent is Antiochus; it serves as the accusative subject of the deponent infinitive, *cōnārī*.

vidēbat: Hannibal is the subject.

nūllā...in rē: *nūllā* is separated from its noun and preposition, *in rē*, for emphasis.

(4) praefuit: > *praèsum* + dative, *paucīs nāvibus* (7.1, 8.4).

iīsque [nāvibus]: ablative of means.

in Āsiam: referring to Asia Minor (i.e., roughly modern day Turkey), as is common in Roman authors.

adversus: preposition + accusative, *classem* (*Rhodiōrum*). Rhodes was a powerful Greek state, known for its superior navy.

in Pamphȳliō marī: Pamphylia is a region between Lycia and Cilicia in southwest Asia Minor. The naval battle was fought near Eurymedon.

quō: connective relative (AG §308f), referring to the battle mentioned in the previous sentence.

cum multitūdine adversāriōrum suī superārentur: concessive *cum clause* (AG §549).

suī: nominative plural, "his (Hannibal's) troops"; a common idiom.

quō cornū: locative ablative; "on the flank [i.e., the section of the battle line] where".

Chapter 9

Hannibal flees to Crete, where he uses a clever ruse to save his money from the treacherous inhabitants.

(1) Antiochō fugātō: ablative absolute. Nepos refers to Antiochus' defeat at the Battle of Magnesia in western Asia Minor in 190 BC. The Roman forces were led by Lucius Cornelius Scipio, the brother of Scipio Africanus. Antiochus subsequently agreed to onerous terms of peace: he renounced his claim to any land in Europe and Anatolia west of the Taurus Mountains, paid a massive indemnity, handed over all of his war elephants, reduced his navy to only 12 warships, and agreed to deliver Hannibal.

nē dēderētur: fear clause dependent on participle, *verēns* (AG §564); *nē* indicates that Hannibal fears the action in the clause, "fearing that he be betrayed".

quod: refers to the action of the preceding clause (*dēderētur*).

accidisset: impersonal, "it would have happened".

sī suī fēcisset potestātem: an idiom, "if he (Hannibal) had provided [Antiochus] the opportunity (*potestātem*) [to meet] him (*suī*)"; *suī*, objective genitive, referring to Hannibal. Hannibal fled first to Armenia, where he was said to have founded the city of Artaxata.

Crētam ad Gortȳniōs vēnit: Crētam: accusative of place to which, usually with a preposition, unlike *domum*, *rūs*, and the names of towns and small islands (AG §427.2). ad Gortȳniōs: "to the Gortynians". Gortyn was an ally of Ptolemaic Egypt and an important city in south–central Crete, near the foot of Mt. Ida. At this time, Crete was riven by conflict between several powerful city–states.

108   Cornelius Nepos, *Life of Hannibal*

ut ibi...cōnsīderāret: purpose clause.

quō: adverb, "to where, whither", introducing indirect question dependent on *cōnsīderāret*.

(2) vir omnium callidissimus: i.e., Hannibal; recall that Nepos characterized Fabius Maximus with the same adjective (5.2).

in magnō sē fore perīculō: indirect statement introduced by *vīdit*; note how Nepos artfully embeds the accusative subject (*sē*) and verb (*fore* = *futūrum esse*, see note on 2.4) within the prepositional phrase, *in magnō...perīculō*.

nisi quid: = *nisi (ali)quid*; see note on 2.6.

propter avāritiam Crētēnsium: explains why Hannibal thought that *in magnō sē fore perīculō*. **Crētēnsium:** genitive plural > *Crētēnsis*.

sēcum: typical for *cum sē*, as whenever *cum* appears with a personal pronoun (e.g. *mēcum, nōbīscum*, etc.).

fāmam: accusative subject of *exīsse*; here, "report" or "rumor" of his *magnam pecūniam*.

11. Hannibal's Ruse of the Amphorae. Drawing by Joelle Cicak, CC BY.

(3) capit...complet...operit: historical presents to convey a sense of lively narrative (AG §469; see note on 4.3).

amphorās: large earthenware vessels with two handles that were used for transport and storage.

plumbō: an ablative of means may be used with verbs and adjectives of "filling, abundance, etc.", *complet* (AG §409a; 11.6); the same construction appears two sentences later: *suā pecūniā complet*.

summās: "the tops" (of the amphorae).

hās: i.e., *amphorās*; on its position before the ablative absolute, *praesentibus prīncipibus*, see note on 8.2.

praesentibus prīncipibus: ablative absolute; since Latin lacks the present or perfect participle of *esse*, an ablative absolute can contain a noun and adjective or two nouns in the ablative (AG §419a).

in templō Diānae: Nepos uses the Roman name of the Greek goddess Artemis.

crēdere: infinitive with an accusative subject, *sē*; "pretending (*simulāns*) to entrust an accusative (*suās fortūnās*) to the dative (*fideī*)"; *fidēs*: not "faith" but "reliability" → "trustworthiness" → "good faith"; compare the derogatory expression *Pūnica fidēs* ("Punic trustworthiness" → "bad faith" → "treachery").

illōrum: i.e., the assembled leaders of the Gortynians (*praesentibus principibus*).

hīs in errōrem inductīs: ablative absolute.

eāsque: i.e., *statuās aeneās*.

domī: genitive limiting *in prōpatulō* rather than locative.

(4) Gortȳniī: subject of *custōdiunt*.

magnā cūrā: ablative of manner.

nōn tam ā cēterīs quam ab Hannibale: correlatives, "not so much from... as from...".

īnscientibus iīs: ablative absolute; *iīs*, i.e., *Gortȳniīs*.

nē...tolleret...dūceret: understand *amphorās* as the object of both verbs in the negative purpose clause; **tolleret...dūceret:** imperfect subjunctives in secondary sequence after a historical present, *custōdiunt* (AG §485e).

Chapter 10

Hannibal arrives at the court of Prusias, King of Bithynia (1), and prepares to fight Eumenes II, an ally of Rome (2–3). He devises a novel biological weapon for use against Eumenes' superior fleet (4–6). The episode with Eumenes is the most detailed in the Life *(10.4–11.6).*

(1) cōnservātīs suīs rēbus and **illūsīs Crētēnsibus omnibus:** Nepos begins this section with two consecutive ablative absolutes. **Poenus:** i.e., Hannibal. **illūsīs:** > *illudō, -ere,* not *ille, illa, illud.*

Prūsiam: Prusias I "The Lame" (ca. 243–182 BC), the king of Bithynia, a kingdom on the southern shore of the Black Sea. It is unclear why Prusias would be in the neighboring kingdom of Pontus when Hannibal met him (*in Pontum*).

apud quem: i.e., Prusias; connective relative (AG §308f).

eōdem animō: ablative of quality (AG §415; see note on 2.5), "of the same mind".

neque aliud quicquam...quam: "and (*ēgit*) nothing other than (*rēgem armāvit*)..."; Hannibal is the subject of the sentence.

(2) quem cum: note that the subordinating *cum* is postponed after the connective relative, which refers to Prusias.

domesticīs opibus: ablative of specification (AG §418; 1.1), indicating the respect in which Prusias was *minus rōbustum*, "too weak".

dissidēbat ab eō Pergamēnus rēx Eumenēs, Rōmānīs amīcissimus: Eumenes II (197–159 BC), the king of Pergamon (*Pergamēnus rēx*) was a staunch ally of Rome (*Rōmānīs amīcissimus*; on the meaning of *amīcitiā*, see note on 2.4). After Antiochus' defeat at Magnesia, the Romans granted Eumenes extensive territory in Asia Minor, bringing him into conflict with Prusias.

    ab eō: i.e., Prusias.

et marī et terrā: correlatively, "both...and"; these ablatives of place are more commonly rendered as *terrā marīque.*

(3) utrobīque: adverb, "on both parts" or "on both sides", i.e., *et marī et terrā*.

quō: connective relative (AG §308f; 8.4, 9.1); "for this reason", i.e., *propter Rōmānōrum societātem*.

Hannibal: nominative subject of *cupiēbat* despite its position within the indirect statement (*eum...opprimī*). Roman authors often juxtapose names and pronouns.

quem: connective relative; its antecedent is *eum*, i.e., Eumenes.

sī remōvisset: pluperfect subjunctive not because Hannibal's assessment of the situation is incorrect but because the protasis appears in indirect speech; Nepos uses the subjunctive because Hannibal originally thought (*arbitrābātur*): "if I eliminate Eumenes (*removerit*, future perfect), everything else will be..."; when Nepos reports the future perfect, *removerit* is rendered as the pluperfect subjunctive, *remōvisset* (AG §589).

ad hunc interficiendum: *ad* + gerundive, expressing purpose, "to kill him" (AG §506).

tālem iniit ratiōnem: "he devised the following plan".

(4) classe: ablative of means.

erant dēcrētūrī: future active periphrastic (AG §195) > *decernō*, "they were about to fight".

superābātur: subject is Hannibal, "he was surpassed by" → "was inferior to", with an ablative of respect, (*nāvium*) *multitūdine*.

dolō erat pugnandum: the neuter indicates that this is the impersonal gerundive (AG §500.3).

cum pār nōn esset armīs: causal *cum* clause, "because...". **armīs:** ablative of respect.

quam plūrimās: "as many as possible" (*quam* + superlative), object of *colligī...que...conicī*.

imperāvit: *imperō* is typically followed by *ut* + subjunctive; here, *imperāvit* introduces an indirect statement: [*eōs*] *colligī...–que...conicī*.

in vāsa fīctilia: "into earthenware vessels"; *vāsa* is neuter plural.

(5) hārum cum effēcisset magnam multitūdinem: circumstantial *cum* clause. **effēcisset:** pluperfect subjunctive in secondary sequence after historical presents, *convocat* and *praecipit* (AG §485e). **hārum:** i.e., *venēnātās serpentēs vīvās*.

diē ipsō: ablative of time when.

factūrus erat: compare to *erant dēcrētūrī* (10.4).

12. Snakes on a Boat. Drawing by Joelle Cicak, CC BY.

convocat...que...praecipit: historical presents to convey a sense of lively narrative (AG §469; see note on 4.3).

iīsque: dative with *praecipit*, substantive purpose clause (AG §563, sometimes called a jussive noun clause), *omnēs ut...concurrant...tantum... habeant sē dēfendere*.

omnēs ut...concurrant: the word order is unusual; again Nepos has positioned a word before the subordinating conjunction for emphasis.

in ūnam...nāvem: an example of hysterologia, or the insertion of words that interrupts the syntactic flow of the sentence; it emphasizes the order that everyone (*omnēs*) attack only Eumenes' ship (*ūnam...nāvem*). **concurrant:** present subjunctive depending on *praecipit*.

ā cēterīs: "against all the other *nāvibus*".

tantum satis habeant: "they should consider it enough" → "should be content". Because *tantus* conveys only the idea of relative greatness, it may also denote a small amount, "just enough".

id: the demonstrative refers to the sense of what came before, i.e., *sē dēfendere*.

illōs...cōnsecūtūrōs [esse]: depends on an implied verb of speaking (e.g., *dīxit*, 12.3).

(6) rēx: subject of *veherētur* in the indirect question introduced by the interrogative adjective *quā*; it has been displaced before its relative clause for additional emphasis.

ut [classiāriī] scīrent: result clause.

sē factūrum [esse]: depends on an implied verb of speaking, like *illōs... consecūtūrōs* (10.5).

magnō iīs pollicētur praemiō fore: a double dative construction dependent on *pollicētur*, "he promises that it will be a (source of) great reward for them" (AG §382). **magnō...praemiō:** dative of purpose with *fore*; **iīs:** dative of reference with *fore*.

Chapter 11

Hannibal lays a trap for Eumenes, who escapes (1–4). Hannibal's biological weapon routs the Pergamene navy (5–6).

(1) tālī cohortātiōne mīlitum factā: ablative absolute. **mīlitum:** objective genitive limiting *cohortātiōne*, "exhortation of the soldiers".

ab utrīsque: i.e., Hannibal and Eumenes II.

114   Cornelius Nepos, *Life of Hannibal*

dēdūcitur and **mittit:** historical presents, see note on *adficitur* (4.3).

quārum: = *nāvium*.

aciē cōnstitūtā: ablative absolute.

priusquam signum pugnae darētur: for the temporal subjunctive, see note on 7.6.

suīs: i.e., Hannibal's men.

quō locō Eumenēs esset: indirect question with *faceret*. **quō locō:** ablative of place.

in scaphā: a skiff or small rowboat.

cum cādūceō: the staff carried by heralds and ambassadors as a symbol of their office and so as a symbol of safe passage to and from enemies.

(2) quī: its antecedent is *tabellārius*.

sē rēgem professus est quaerere: *professus est* introduces the indirect statement, *sē rēgem...quaerere*. Word order in this sentence is determined by an intelligible set of stylistic preferences: the first word in the phrase, *sē*, refers to the subject of the previous clause; *rēgem* follows because of the Roman preference for juxtaposing personal nouns; then *professus est*, because the verb introducing the indirect statement has a tendency to come before the verb in the indirect statement, *quaerere*.

quod nēmō dubitābat: the indicative reveals that this is Nepos' own assessment of the situation, not necessarily that of Eumenes or his sailors (compare 1.1).

quīn...esset scrīptum: *quīn* often introduces subjunctive clauses after expressions of hindering, resisting, and doubting (*nēmō dubitābat*, AG §558), "because no one was doubting that (*quīn*)...".

ducis nāve dēclārātā suīs: ablative absolute. **ducis:** i.e., Eumenes. Note how Nepos places the genitive, *ducis*, before the noun it limits, *nāve*, in order to juxtapose it with *tabellārius*. **suīs:** dative with *dēclārātā*, i.e., "to his own men".

eōdem: i.e., *eōdem* [*locō*], specified by the subsequent clause, *unde erat ēgressus*.

(3) solūtā epistulā: ablative absolute. **solūtā:** i.e., by breaking the wax seal on the letter.

quae ad irrīdendum eum pertinērent: *quae* is neuter plural because a plural is implied by the main clause (*nihil in eā repperit*). **ad irrīdendum eum:** gerundive indicating purpose (see note on 10.3).

cuius: connective relative; its antecedent must be *epistulā*.

dubitāvit: on the use of *dubitō* + infinitive, see note on 2.4.

(4) ūniversī: "all at once", modifies *Bīthȳniī*. Note how Nepos embeds the ablative of cause, (*Hannibalis*) *praeceptō*, within the noun–adjective phrase to emphasize why the *Bīthȳniī* attacked *ūniversī* (12.4, 13.2).

adoriuntur: "fell upon".

quōrum vim rēx cum sustinēre nōn posset: by now Nepos' tendency to postpone the subordinating conjunction, *cum*, after words that associate the clause with elements of the preceeding sentence, should be familiar; also 11.5, below.

fugā: ablative of means.

quam: antecedent is *salūtem*.

intrā sua praesidia: i.e., Eumenes' fortified naval encampment (*ad sua castra nautica* in 11.6). Ancient warships were built for speed and maneuverability. Because they were unstable in foul weather and lacked accommodations for their crews, sailors tended to make camp on land at night.

(5) eās: i.e., *Pergamēnās nāvēs*.

vāsa fīctilia: the subject of *conicī coepta sunt*.

dē quibus suprā mentiōnem fēcimus: Nepos first introduced the earthenware jars in 10.4. **fēcimus:** ancient authors often used plural forms to refer to themselves, especially in prose (see note on 3.1).

coepta sunt: the passive of the defective verb *coepī* is often used with passive verbs (AG §205a), "they began to be thrown (*conicī*)".

quae iacta: "these (*vāsa fictilia*) having been thrown".

initiō: ablative of time, "at first".

concitārunt: = *concitā(vē)runt*, syncopated perfect (AG §181), "arouse, excite, cause" something (accusative, *rīsum*) in someone (dative, *pugnantibus*).

quā rē id fieret: indirect question, dependent on *poterat intellegī*; **quā rē:** = *quārē*.

(6) serpentibus: an ablative of means may be used with verbs and adjectives of "filling, abundance, etc.", *opplētās* (AG §409a).

novā rē: ablative of means. **novā:** "strange, unusual, unprecedented", as often in Latin.

perterritī: perfect passive participle, agreeing with implicit subject of *vertērunt*.

quid potissimum vītārent: indirect question introduced by *cum...nōn vidērent*; i.e., the Pergamene sailors were in confusion whether they should rid themselves of the snakes or continue to attack Prusias' ships. **potissimum:** adverb, "first of all, especially, in preference to all".

puppēs vertērunt: *puppēs*, literally "sterns", refers by synecdoche to the entire ship; compare the idiom *terga vertere*, "turn (their) backs", i.e., retreat.

(7) cōnsiliō: i.e., his ingenious use of snakes. Nepos often contrasts ingenuity (*cōnsilium*) with brute force (*arma*).

neque tum sōlum, sed saepe aliās: "not only at that time...but often at other times..."; a variation on the common correlative construction, *nōn sōlum... sed etiam* (6.4, 7.5); **aliās:** adverb, "in other places, times" (AG §215.3).

pedestribus cōpiīs: ablative of instrument, "with infantry" → "in land battles".

parī prūdentiā: ablative of manner (AG §412; 12.4); Nepos introduced tactical brilliance (*prūdentiā*) as Hannibal's defining characteristic in 1.1.

Chapter 12

Romans demand that Hannibal be surrendered (1–3). When Hannibal discovers that he is surrounded by his enemies, he commits suicide (4–5).

(1) quae: connective relative (AG §308f).

geruntur: historical present, see note on *adficitur* (4.3).

accidit cāsū: impersonal, "it happened by chance"; its subject is furnished by the substantive clause, *ut lēgātī Prūsiae...cēnārent.*

Rōmae: locative.

apud T. Quinctium Flāminīnum cōnsulārem: "at the house of..."; **cōnsulārem:** "ex-consul". Titus Quinctius Flamininus (ca. 229–ca. 174 BC) defeated Philip V of Macedon at the Battle of Cynocephalae in 197 BC, ending Macedonian domination of Greece. The following year Flamininus appeared at the Isthmian Games and flamboyantly declared that the Greeks were free from foreign domination. Fifty years later Greece was reduced to a Roman province after Rome defeated the Achaean League at the Battle of Corinth in 146 BC, the same year that Rome destroyed Carthage.

dē Hannibale mentiōne factā: ablative absolute that includes the prepositional phrase, *dē Hannibale.*

ex iīs ūnus: partitive, "one of them", i.e., the *lēgātī Prūsiae.*

eum: i.e., Hannibal.

(2) senātuī: dative with the compound verb, *dētulit,* "he communicated".

patrēs cōnscrīptī: "enrolled fathers", the standard appellation for Roman senators.

quī...existimārent: relative clause of characteristic indicating cause (AG §535e), "because they judged...".

Hannibale vīvō: ablative absolute; since Latin lacks the present or perfect participle of *esse,* an ablative absolute can contain a noun and adjective or two nouns in the ablative (AG §419a).

in iīs Flāminīnum: "Flamininus (was included) among these" (i.e., the Roman legates).

quī ab rēge peterent: relative clause of purpose, "in order to ask…".

inimīcissimum: "greatest enemy"; object of both *habēret* and *dēderet*.

suum and **sibi:** indirect reflexives (AG §300.2) because they refer to the words or thoughts of those making the demand (*lēgātī*). **sēcum:** a direct reflexive referring to Prusias, the subject of its own clause (AG §300.1). Both uses of the reflexive are standard; the situation—who has Hannibal and to whom he must be given—prevents confusion.

sibique dēderet: *ut* is not necessary because *–que* continues the indirect command introduced by *nē*; the singular subject of *habēret* and *dēderet* must be Prusias (*ab rēge*).

(3) negāre: "to give a negative answer", with a dative, *hīs* [*lēgātīs*].

illud: emphatic; it agrees with the substantive purpose clause that follows, *nē id ā sē fierī postulārent* (AG §563, sometimes called a jussive noun clause); *postulārent* usually expects a substantive purpose clause but Nepos uses the accusative + infinitive to avoid a confusing ut immediately after *nē*.

ā sē: indirect reflexive, see note above on *suum* and *sibi*.

quod: relative pronoun; its antecedent is *id*.

adversus iūs hospitiī: for the Romans, hospitality (*hospitium*) or the proper treatment of guests (*hospitēs*) was among the stongest bonds between individuals. Romans considered a violation of *hospitium* to be a great impiety and the protection due a guest was often deemed greater than that due blood relatives. Prusias, therefore, in appealing to the *iūs hospitiī*, is not merely citing etiquette, but evoking one of the most fundamental and universally recognized social conventions of the ancient world. Compare the biblical story of Lot, who offered his virgin daughters to a drunken crowd that was demanding two guests whom Lot had just met.

ipsī: i.e., the *lēgātī Rōmānī*.

ubi esset: subject is Hannibal.

inventūrōs [esse]: depends on an implied verb of saying (e.g., *Prusias dīxit*; 10.5, 10.6).

ūnō locō: when the ablative of place appears with an adjective, the preposition (*in*) is often omitted; compare *in Italiā*, but *tōtā Italiā*.

mūnerī: dative of purpose, used to show what a thing accomplishes, "as a gift"; often with a dative of the person affected, *eī* (AG §382).

idque sīc aedificā(ve)rat, ut...exitūs habēret: result clause signaled by *sīc*; *exitūs* is accusative plural.

nē ūsū venīret, quod accidit: fear clause dependent on *verēns*. **ūsū venīret:** idiom, "it happens, occurs", especially common in Nepos and his contemporary Cicero. **quod accidit:** the relative clause serves as subject of *venīret*.

13. Hannibal Surrounded. Drawing by Joelle Cicak, CC BY.

(4) puer: often used for "slave" without reference to age.

plūrēs praeter cōnsuētūdinem armātōs: Nepos embeds a prepositional phrase, *praeter cōnsuētūdinem* ("more than was usual"), within the noun–adjective phrase that it modifies.

quī imperāvit eī: introducing the substantive clause of purpose, *ut... circumīret ac properē sibi nuntiāret* (AG §563). **quī:** connective relative; its antecedent must be Hannibal (a slave would not be giving orders to the general). **eī:** i.e., the slave; dative with *imperāvit*.

num...obsidērētur: in indirect questions, *num* does not expect a negative answer, as it does in direct questions.

eōdem modō: ablative of manner.

(5) puer: the subject of the circumstantial cum clause (*cum...renūntiāsset... que...ostendisset*) is shifted before the subordinating conjunction.

omnīsque: *–īs* is a common alternative spelling of the accusative plural of i–stem nouns (AG §77) and adjectives (AG §115–121). **sēnsit:** subject is Hannibal; introduces three indirect statements:
  a) *id nōn...factum [esse]*,
  b) *sed sē petī*,
  c) *neque...vītam esse retinendam*.

fortuītō: adverb, "by chance".

sē: reflexive, referring to Hannibal.

sibi: dative of agent with the periphrastic, *esse retinendam*.

quam nē aliēnō arbitriō dīmitteret: negative purpose clause. **quam:** connective relative; its antecedent is *vītam*. **aliēnō arbitriō:** "by another's will".

memor: "mindful of" + objective genitive, *prīstinārum virtūtum* (AG §347–348).

venēnum: the Roman satirist Juvenal records that Hannibal kept the poison in a ring (*Satire* 10.164: "but a little ring was the redeemer of Cannae and avenger of so much blood", *sed ille Cannārum vindex ac tantī sanguinis ultor, anulus*). According to other accounts, Hannibal had a slave strangle him with his military cloak, or he drank bull's blood, which was thought to congeal so quickly that it would suffocate the drinker (Plutarch, *Life of Flamininus* 20). His great rival, Scipio Africanus, may have died in the same year.

cōnsuē(ve)rat: syncopated perfect (AG §181).

Chapter 13

The year of Hannibal's death is disputed (1). Nepos discusses his sources (2–3). The conclusion of the Life *and the announcement of Nepos' next project (4).*

(1) perfūnctus: > *perfungor* + ablative, *multīs variīsque labōribus*.

annō acquiēvit septuāgēsimō: Hannibal was actually in his sixties. Like most traditional cultures, Romans routinely used round numbers even when a specific number might be discovered.

quibus cōnsulibus interierit: indirect question with *nōn convēnit*, "it is not agreed under which consuls…"; the three dates given are 183, 182, and 181 BC.

M. Claudiō Marcellō Q. Fabiō Labeōne cōnsulibus: i.e., in 183 BC, the date given by Atticus (the historian and friend of Cicero) in his now-lost *Liber annalis* (*in Annālī suō*). This is the most likely date.

scrīptum relīquit: "left it written" → "wrote". For the periphrasis, see note on 8.2.

Sulpicius Blithō: a contemporary of Nepos; Blitho, whose account is lost, gave 182 BC as the date of Hannibal's death.

Polybius: the famed Greek historian (ca. 200–118 BC) gives the consuls of 181 BC.

(2) hic tantus: in this combination, favored by Roman authors, *tantus* is equivalent to *magnus* or another honorific.

temporis: partitive genitive with *nōn nihil*, "not no time" → "some time".

litterīs: dative of purpose; i.e., "literature" or "literary studies".

sunt: "there are" → "there survive".

in iīs: i.e., "among them".

ad Rhodiōs dē...gestīs: this is a title: "(Address) to the Rhodians..." They had joined Gnaeus Manilius Volso on campaign (*rēbus gestīs*) against the Galatians of Asia Minor (*in Asiā*) in 189 BC. The work does not survive.

(3) huius: i.e., Hannibal; *huius* does not agree with *bellī*, but instead limits the phrase *bellī gesta*.

bellī gesta: "the deeds of war", in contrast to literature, a pursuit of peace.

multī: subject of *prōdidērunt*.

memoriae: dative with *prōdidērunt*, "transmit (accusative, *gesta*) to (dative, *memoriae*)" → "commemorate, put forth in writing".

quam diū fortūna passa est: "for as long as fortune allowed".

Sīlēnus et Sōsylus Lacedaemonius: precious little survives of the works by these authors, who were essential sources for subsequent historians, including Polybius and Livy. The history by Silenus, an ethnic Greek from Cale Acte in Sicily, was respected by Polybius and widely cited by Roman authors, including Cicero, who called his history "a thoroughly reliable authority on Hannibal's life and achievements" (*De divinatione* 1.49). Sosylus the Spartan accompanied Hannibal on his campaign and composed a *Hannibalica*, a history of the Second Punic War in seven books. Polybius condemned it as "the common gossip of a barber's shop" (3.20.5).

hōc Sōsylō: in apposition with *doctōre*.

litterārum Graecārum: objective genitive limiting *doctōre*, "teacher of Greek literature".

ūsus est: governs an ablative of means, *doctōre* (AG §410).

(4) nōs: i.e., Nepos; accusative subject of the indirect statement introduced by *tempus est*.

quō facilius...possit iūdicārī: relative clause of purpose, "by which..." (AG §531), on which the indirect question, *quī virī praeferendī sint*, depends.

collātīs utrōrumque factīs: ablative absolute. **utrōrumque:** "of both", i.e., "of the foreign and the Roman generals". Nepos' biographies of Roman generals are lost.

Full Vocabulary for Nepos' *Life of Hannibal* and *Prologus* to the *Lives of Outstanding Commanders*[1]

— A —

ā ab abs: from, by (+abl.) (18)

abiciō –icere –iēcī –iectus: throw down, toss (1)

absēns absentis: absent (3)

absum abesse āfuī: be away, absent (1)

ac: and, and besides, than (6)

accēdō –cēdere –cessī –cessum: approach (1)

accidō –cidere –cidī: happen; fall (3)

accipiō –cipere –cēpī –ceptum: receive (2)

ācer ācris ācre: sharp, piercing (2)

aciēs aciēī f.: edge; line of battle (3)

acquiēscō –quiēscere –quiēvī –quiētum: die, repose in death (1)

---

[1] **Nota bene:** the frequency of each word in the *Life of Hannibal* appears in parentheses. Chapter and other vocabulary lists available at the Dickinson Classics website, http://dcc.dickinson.edu/nepos-hannibal/vocabulary-texts-and-maps; customizable vocablulary lists can be made at http://bridge.haverford.edu

© Bret Mulligan, CC BY 4.0   http://dx.doi.org/10.11647/OBP.0068.08

ad: to, towards, at (+acc.) (18)

addūcō –dūcere –dūxī –ductum: lead to, induce (2)

adeō –īre –iī –itum: go to (1)

adeō: to such a degree, so (1)

adhibeō –hibēre –hibuī –hibitus: apply

afficiō –ficere –fēcī –fectum: affect, visit with (+abl.) (1)

adiungō –iungere –iūnxī –iūnctum: add, connect, join to (2)

admīror –mīrārī –mīrātus sum: wonder (at), be surprised

adorior –orīrī –ortus sum: assault, approach (as an enemy) (1)

adulēscentulus –ī m.: young man, youth

adversārius –a –um: opposite, hostile, contrary (4)

adversus: facing, opposite, against, opposed (to) (+acc.) (6)

aedēs aedis f.: building; house (in pl.)

aedificium –ī n.: building (2)

aedificō –āre: build, erect (1)

Aemilius –ī m.: Aemilius (2)

aēneus –a –um: made of copper or bronze (1)

aequus –a –um: equal (1)

aerārius –a –um: of or belonging to copper or bronze; treasury (pl.) (1)

aetās aetātis f.: age, time of life (2)

afficiō –ficere –fēcī –fectum: affect, visit with (+abl.) (1)

Āfrica –ae f.: Africa (3)

ager agrī m.: field (1)

agō agere ēgī āctum: drive, do, act (3)

aliēnus –a –um: foreign, strange (2)

aliquis –quae –quod: some, any; **si quis, si quid:** anyone who, anything that (1)

aliquot: several, some (3)

aliter: otherwise, differently

alius alia aliud: other, another (5)

Alpēs Alpium f.: Alps (1)

Alpicus –ī m.: inhabitant of the Alps (1)

alter altera alterum: other of two (1)

amātor amātōris m.: lover, friend

amīcitia –ae f.: friendship, alliance (1)

amīcus –a –um: friendly (2)

amphora –ae f.: amphora (large, two–handled jar) (1)

amplus –a –um: large, spacious (1)

angustus –a –um: narrow, confined (1)

anima –ae f.: breath, spirit (1)

animus –ī m.: spirit, mind (2)

annālis annālis m.: record of events, chronicle (1)

annus –ī m.: year (7)

annuus –a –um: for a year, annual (1)

ante: before, in front of (adv. and prep. +acc.) (1)

anteā: before, earlier, already (2)

antecēdō –cēdere –cessī –cessum: go before, precede, excel (1)

Antiochus –ī m.: Antiochus (III, the Great, king of Syria) (6)

appāreō –pārēre –pāruī: appear, become visible (1)

apparō –āre: prepare (1)

appellō –āre: call, address, name (1)

Appennīnus –ī m.: Apennines (mountain range running the length of the Italian peninsula) (1)

apud: near, in the presence of (+acc.) (13)

Āpulia –ae f.: Apulia (region in southeastern Italy) (1)

āra –ae f.: altar (1)

arbitrium -ī n.: decision, judgment, authority (1)

arbitror arbitrārī arbitrātus sum: consider, think (1)

argentum -ī n.: silver, money (1)

arma -ōrum n. pl.: arms, weapons, armor, tools (3)

armō -āre: arm, equip with weapons (2)

ascendō -scendere -scendī -scēnsum: climb up, ascend (1)

Āsia -ae f.: Asia (3)

at: but, but yet (3)

Athēniēnsis Athēniēnsis m.: Athenian

atque: and in addition, and also, and (7)

Atticus -ī m.: Atticus (1)

audeō audēre ausus sum: dare, be eager (2)

Aurēlius -ī m.: Aurelius (1)

aureus -a -um: golden; splendid (1)

aurum -ī n.: gold (1)

aut: or (2)

autem: moreover, but, however (6)

avāritia -ae f.: greed, rapacity (1)

— B —

Baebius -ī m.: Baebius (2)

bellicōsus -a -um: warlike, fierce (1)

bellō -āre: wage war, fight, contend (2)

bellum -ī n.: war (12)

bene: well (1)

bīduum -ī n.: two day period (1)

bīnī -ae -a: in pairs (1)

Bīthȳnia -ae f.: Bithynia (a kingdom in northern Asia Minor) (1)

Bīthȳnius –ī m.: inhabitant of Bithynia (1)

Blithō Blithōnis m.: Blitho (1)

bonus –a –um: goods, property (1)

— C —

cādūceus –ī m.: herald's staff (1)

callidus –a –um: clever, cunning, shrewd (2)

campus –ī m.: plain, field (1)

Cannēnsis Cannēnse: of Cannae (town in southeastern Italy) (1)

cantō –āre: play (an instrument), sing

capiō capere cēpī captum: seize (2)

captīvus –ī m.: captive (2)

Capua –ae f.: Capua (city southeast of Rome) (1)

castellum –ī n.: fort, fortress (1)

castrum –ī n.: fortress, camp (regularly plural) (5)

cāsus cāsūs m.: a fall; chance, accident (1)

causa –ae f.: cause, reason; **causā:** (+ preceding gen.) for the sake of (1)

celēbritās celēbritātis f.: crowd, company, society

celer celeris celere: swift; adv. **celeriter** (1)

cēlō –āre: hide, conceal (1)

cēna –ae f.: dinner, supper

cēnō –āre: dine (1)

Centēnius –ī m.: Centenius (1)

cēterus –a –um: the others, the rest (6)

Cethēgus –ī m.: Cethegus (1)

Cīmōn Cīmōnis m.: Cimon

circiter: near, not far from (1)

circumdō –dare –dedī –datum: surround, encircle (1)

circumeō –īre –iī/–īvī –itum: surround (1)

circumveniō –venīre –vēnī –ventum: surround, encircle (1)

citō –āre: announce, call on

cīvis civis m./f.: citizen (1)

cīvitās cīvitātis f.: citizenship, state (1)

clam: secretly (1)

clandestīnus –a –um: secret, hidden, concealed (1)

classiārius –ī m.: mariner; (pl.) naval forces, marines (1)

classis classis f.: class, division, fleet (3)

Clastidium –ī n.: Clastidium (town in northern Italy) (1)

Claudius –ī m.: Claudius (3)

claudō claudere clausī clausum: close, shut (1)

coepī coepisse coeptus: begin (2)

cōgitō –āre: think, reflect (1)

cognātiō cognātiōnis f.: kinship, blood–relationship

cōgnōscō –gnōscere –gnōvī –gnitum: learn, understand (1)

cohortātiō cohortātiōnis f.: exhortation (1)

collēga –ae m.: colleague (1)

colligō –ere –lēgī –lēctum: gather together, collect (2)

colloquium –ī n.: conversation (1)

commemorō –āre: recall, mention (1)

committō –mittere –mīsī –missum: join, entrust to (+dat.); perform, do (1)

commodus –a –um: proper, elegant

comparō –āre: get ready, provide; compare (1)

comperiō –perīre –perī –pertum: find out, learn, know (1)

compleō –plēre –plēvī –plētum: fill up (2)

complūrēs complūrium: several (1)

compōnō –pōnere pōsuī pōsitum: build, construct, arrange (2)

comprehendō –prehendere –prehendī –prehensum: seize, apprehend (2)

comprobō –āre: approve fully, endorse (1)

concīdō –cīdere –cīdī –cīsum: cut to pieces, beat severely, destroy (1)

conciliō –āre: unite, win over (1)

concitō –āre: rouse, excite (1)

concurrō –currere –currī –cursum: join battle with (1)

concursus concursūs m.: meeting, collision, encounter (1)

condīciō condīciōnis f.: agreement, condition (1)

condūcō –dūcere –dūxī –ductus: hire, employ

cōnferō cōnferre contulī collātum: collect, bring to (2)

cōnficiō –ficere –fēcī –fectum: complete, accomplish; destroy, kill, consume (2)

conflīgō –flīgere –flīxī –flīctum: clash, fight (4)

congredior –gredī –gressus sum: come together, meet, join battle (2)

coniciō –icere –iēcī –iectum: cast, fling, toss (2)

coniūnctus –a –um: connected, related

conlocō –āre: place, station, set up (1)

cōnor cōnārī cōnātus sum: try, undertake, attempt (3)

cōnscrībō –scrībere –scrīpsī –scrīptum: enlist; **patrēs cōnscrīptī:** senators (1)

cōnsequor –sequī –secūtus sum: follow up, overtake, attain (3)

cōnserō –serere –seruī –sertum: engage (in close combat), join (battle) (1)

cōnservō –āre: retain, maintain, preserve (3)

cōnsīderō –āre: consider (1)

cōnsilium –ī n.: plan; council, group of advisors (5)

cōnspiciō –spicere –spexī –spectus: catch sight of, perceive (1)

cōnstituō –stituere –stituī –stitūtum: establish, put together (1) cōnsuēscō –suēscere –suēvī –suētum: be accustomed (1)

cōnsuētūdō cōnsuētūdinis f.: custom, habit (1)

cōnsul cōnsulis m.: consul (13)

cōnsulāris cōnsulāre: consular, of consular rank (2)

cōnsultum –ī n.: decree, resolution (1)

contrā: against, opposite (adv. and prep. +acc.)

contrahō –trahere –trāxī –tractum: draw together, assemble, muster (1)

conveniō –venīre –vēnī –ventum: assemble, meet; agree (3)

convīvium –ī n.: banquet, feast

convocō –āre: call together, assemble (1)

cōpia –ae f.: abundance; (pl.) troops (2)

Cornēlius –ī m.: Cornelius (3)

cornū cornūs n.: horn (2)

corōna –ae f.: crown (1)

corrumpō –rumpere –rūpī –ruptum: break up, destroy, ruin (1)

crēdō crēdere crēdidī crēditum: believe (1)

creō –āre: produce, create; elect, choose (1)

Crēta –ae f.: Crete (1)

Crētēnsis Crētēnse: Cretan (2)

cum: with (prep. +abl.); when, since, although (conj. +subj.) (48)

cūnctus –a –um: entire, all together (1)

cupiditās cupiditātis f.: longing, desire, passion (1)

cupiō cupere cupīvī cupītum: desire (2)

cūra –ae f.: care, concern (1)

custōdiō custōdīre custōdīvī custōdītus: guard (1)

Cȳrēnaeus –ī m.: inhabitant of Cyrene (a city in north Africa) (1)

— D —

dē: down from, about, concerning (+abl.) (10)

dēbeō dēbēre dēbuī dēbitum: owe, be obliged (1)

dēbilitō –āre: weaken, impair (1)

dēcernō –cernere –crēvī –crētum: determine, decide (2)

dēclārō –āre: indicate, reveal (1)

decōrus –a –um: proper, suitable

dēdō –dere –didī –ditum: hand over, deliver (2)

dēdūcō –dūcere –dūxī –ductum: launch, lead away (2)

dēfendō –fendere –fendī –fēnsum: defend, ward off (2)

dēferō –ferre –tulī –lātum: carry away, report (3)

deinde or dein: then, next (1)

dēligō –ligere –lēgī –lēctum: choose, select (1)

dēpōnō –pōnere –posuī –positum: lay down, put down (2)

dēserō –serere –seruī –sertum: leave, desert, abandon (1)

dēsistō –sistere –stitī –stitus: cease (from), leave off, abandon (+infin.) (1)

dēspērō –āre: be hopeless, give up (1)

dētrīmentum –ī n.: harm, loss (1)

dēvincō –vincere –vīcī –vīctum: conquer, overcome (1)

dexter dextra dextrum: right; **dextera –ae f.:** right hand (1)

Diāna –ae f.: Diana, a Roman goddess (1)

dīcō dīcere dīxī dictum: say; **causam dīcere:** plead a case; **diem dīcere:** appoint a day (5)

dictātor dictātōris m.: dictator (2)

diēs diēī m./f.: day (7)

dīgnus –a –um: worthy

dīligentia –ae f.: care, diligence (1)

dīligō –ligere –lēxī –lēctum: choose, cherish, love (1)

dīmicō –āre –āvī/uī –ātus: fight (1)

dīmittō –mittere –mīsī –missum: send away (3)

discēdō –cēdere –cessī –cessum: go away, depart (1)

discō discere didicī: learn

disiciō –icere –iēcī –iectum: destroy, scatter (1)

dispālor –pālārī –pālātus sum: to wander around, straggle (1)

dissideō –sidēre –sēdī –sessum: disagree, quarrel (1)

distringō –stringere –strinxī –strictum: distract, be busy (1)

diū: for a long time (2)

dīvīnus –a –um: divine (1)

dō dare dedī datum: give (9)

doceō docēre docuī doctum: teach

doctor doctōris m.: teacher, instructor (1)

dolus –ī m.: artifice, device, trick (2)

domesticus –a –um: personal, private, domestic (1)

domus –ī m.: house, home (6)

dōnō –āre: present with a gift (+acc. of person and abl. of thing) (1)

dubitō –āre: hesitate, doubt (4)

dubius –a –um: doubtful; **sine dubiō**: without a doubt, certainly (2)

dūcō dūcere: dūxī ductum: lead; **uxōrem dūcere**: marry (4)

dum: while (+indic.); until (+subj.); provided that (+subj.) **(2)**

duo duae duo: two (4)

duplex duplicis: double (1)

dux ducis m./f.: leader, general (1)

— E —

efficiō –ficere –fēcī –fectum: bring about, complete; render (+*ut* + subj.) (3)

effugiō –fugere –fūgī –fugitum: escape (1)

ego meī mihi mē mē: I, me, we, us (9)

ēgredior –gredī –gressus sum: stride out, depart, disembark from (+abl.) (2)

elephantus –ī m.: elephant (1)

enim: for, indeed (4)

ēnumerō –āre: enumerate, recount (1)

eō īre iī/īvī itum: go (1)

Epamīnōndās –ae m.: Epaminondas

epistula –ae f.: letter (2)

eques equitis m.: horseman, knight (1)

equitātus equitātūs m.: cavalry (1)

ergā: towards, in relation to (+acc.) (2)

error errōris m.: wandering; error, mistake (1)

et: and (15)

etiam: also, even (4)

Etrūria –ae f.: Etruria (region in Italy, northwest of Rome) (1)

etsī: although (2)

Eumenēs Eumenis m.: Eumenes (II, king of Pergamum in Asia Minor) (7)

ex ē: out of, from (+abl.) (10)

excēdō –cēdere –cessī –cessum: leave, withdraw (1)

excellēns excellentis: distinguished, excellent

exciō –īre –īvī –itum: dispatch, call, incite (1)

exeō –īre –iī –itum: go forth (1)

exerceō –ercēre –ercuī –ercitum: train, exercise, carry on (1) exercitus exercitūs m.: army (10)

exhauriō –haurīre –hausī –haustum: exhaust, deplete (1)

exīstimō –āre: think, believe (1)

exitus exitūs m.: exit (2)

exōrdior –ōrdīrī –ōrsus sum: begin, commence

expediō –pedīre –pedīvī –pedītum: extricate, set free (1)

expers expertis: lacking of, without (+gen.)

explicō –āre: unfold, explain (1)

explōrō –āre: investigate, inquire, put to the test (1)

explicō –āre: unfold, explain

expōnō –pōnere –posuī –positum: set forth, explain

exposcō –poscere –poposcī: demand (1)

expugnō –āre: take by assault, storm (1)

exsul exsulis m./f.: exile (1)

extrā: outside (+acc.) (1)

— F —

Fabius –ī m.: Fabius (3)

facilis facile: easy (4)

faciō facere fēcī factum: do, make (20)

facultās facultātis f.: willingness, readiness (1)

Falernus –ī m.: Falernus (region in Campania, south of Rome) (1)

fāma –ae f.: rumor, fame (1)

familia –ae f.: household, family

ferē: almost

ferō ferre tulī lātum: bear, carry, endure (1)

festīnātiō festīnātiōnis f.: haste, speed, hurry

fictilis fictile: made of clay, earthen (2)

fidēs fideī f.: trust, faith (3)

fīdūcia –ae f.: trust, confidence (1)

fīlius fīliī m.: son (2)

fīnis fīnis m.: end, boundary (2)

fīō fierī factus sum: happen, be done, become (2)

Flāminīnus –ī m.: Flamininus (3)

Flāminius –ī m.: Flaminius (1)

foederō –āre: make an alliance or treaty (1)

foedus foederis n.: treaty (1)

fore: futūrum esse; forem, forēs, foret, forent = essem, essēs, esset, essent: be, exist, live (5)

foris foris f.: door (1)

forte: by chance (1)

fortis forte: brave (1)

fortitūdō fortitūdinis f.: strength, force, manliness (1)

fortuītō: by chance (1)

fortūna –ae f.: fortune (2)

frāter frātris m.: brother (4)

Fregellae –ārum f.: Fregellae (town in Latium, near Rome) (1)

frūstrā: in vain, to no end (1)

frūstror frūstrārī frūstrātus sum: disappoint, frustrate (1)

fuga –ae f.: flight, route (3)

fugō –āre: put to flight (5)

fundāmentum –ī n.: foundation (1)

Fūrius –ī m.: Furius (1)

futūrum esse; forem, forēs, foret, forent = essem, essēs, esset, essent: be, exist, live (6)

— G —

Gāius –ī m.: Gaius (4)

Gallia –ae f.: Gaul (1)

Geminus –ī m.: Geminus (1)

gēns gentis f.: family, clan (2)

genus generis n.: origin, lineage, kind (1)

germānus –a –um: (of a sibling) with the same father

gerō gerere gessī gestum: bear, manage; **bellum gerere:** wage war (8)

Gnaeus –ī m.: Gnaeus (3)

Gortȳnius –ī m.: inhabitant of Gortyn (a city in Crete) (2)

Gracchus –ī: Gracchus (1)

Graecus –a –um: Greek (2)

Grāius –a –um: Greek, Grecian (2)

grātia –ae f.: favor, influence, gratitude (1)

grātus –a –um: pleasant; grateful (2)

gravis grave: heavy, serious (1)

gynaecōnītis gynaecōnītidis f.: women's apartments

— H —

habeō habēre habuī habitum: have, hold (6)

Hadrūmētum –ī n.: Hadrumetum (city in north Africa, near Carthage) (2)

Hamilcar Hamilcaris m.: Hamilcar Barca (Carthaginian general and father of Hannibal) (2)

Hannibal Hannibalis m.: Hannibal (21)

Hasdrubal Hasdrubalis m.: Hasdrubal (brother–in–law of Hannibal) (2)

Hercules Herculis m.: Hercules (1)

hērēditās hērēditātis f.: inheritance (1)

hic haec hoc: this, these (35)

hīc: here (1)

Hispānia –ae f.: Spain (4)

hodiē: today (1)

homō hominis m.: human being (1)

honestās honestātis f.: respectfulness, honor, integrity

honestus –a –um: worthy; decent; honorable

hospitium –ī n.: hospitality (1)

hostia –ae f.: victim, sacrifice (1)

hostis hostis m./f.: stranger, foreigner, enemy (1)

hūc: to this place (3)

humilis humile: low, base

— I —

iaciō iacere iēcī iactum: throw, hurl (1)

iam: now; already (2)

iānua –ae f.: door (1)

ibi: there (4)

īdem eadem idem: the same (8)

igitur: therefore (1)

ille illa illud: that (7)

illūdō –lūdere –lūsī –lūsum: deceive, mock, trick (1)

immittō –mittere –mīsī –missum: send in (1)

immolō –āre: sacrifice, offer as sacrifice (1)

imperātor imperātōris m.: commander (6)

imperium –ī n.: command, power (4)

imperō –āre: command, control (2)

impraesentiārum: at present (1)

imprūdēns imprūdentis: unaware, lacking foresight, imprudent (1)

in: (+acc.) to, into (+abl.) at, in, on (62)

incendō –cendere –cendī –cēnsum: inflame, set fire to (2)

incola –ae m./f.: inhabitant (1)

incrēdibilis incrēdibile: unbelievable, incredible (1)

inde: from there, from then (2)

indigeō –digēre –diguī: be in need of, require (+gen.) (1)

indūcō –dūcere –dūxī –ductum: lead in, entice (3)

ineō –īre –iī –itum: go into, begin, undertake (1)

inermis inerme: unarmed (1)

īnfāmis īnfāme: dishonorable, disgraceful

īnferō īnferre intulī illātum: bring in, introduce, bring to, carry in (1)

īnfitior –fitiārī –fitiātus sum: deny, contradict (1)

iniciō –icere –iēcī –iectum: inspire, cause, put in (1)

inimīcus –a –um: unfriendly (2)

initium –ī n.: beginning (1)

inquam, inquis, inquit, inquiunt: say (used with direct speech) (2)

īnsciēns īnscientis: ignorant, unaware (1)

īnsidiae –ārum f.: ambush (3)

īnsidior –ārī –ātus sum: ambush, lay a trap (+dat.) (1)

īnstituō –stituere –stituī –stitūtum: undertake; equip (2)

īnstitūtum –ī n.: practice, custom

intellegō –legere –lēxī –lēctum: understand (2)

inter: between, among; during (+acc.) (1)

intereō –īre –iī –itum: perish, die (1)

interficiō –ficere –fēcī –fectum: kill (5)

interior interius: inner, more inward (1)

interitus interitūs m.: ruin, destruction (1)

intrā: within (+acc.) (1)

inveniō –venīre –vēnī –ventum: find; discover (1)

invictus –a –um: undefeated (1)

invidia –ae f.: envy, jealousy, hatred (1)

ipse –a –um: him– her– itself (9)

irrīdeō –rīdēre –rīsī –rīsum: mock, make fun of (1)

is ea id: he, she, it (69)

ita: thus, so (2)

Italia –ae f.: Italy (8)

itaque: and so, therefore (1)

item: likewise (1)

iter itineris n.: journey, route (3)

iterum: again (2)

iubeō iubēre iussī iussum: bid, order (2)

iūdicō –āre: judge, decide (2)

Iuppiter Iovis m.: Jupiter (1)

iūrō –āre: take an oath, swear; **iūs iūrandum:** oath (1)

iūs iūris n.: right, justice, law (1)

iūs iūrandum n.: oath (1)

iuvencus –ī m.: bull (1)

— K —

Karthāginiēnsis Karthāginiēnsis: Carthaginian (5)

Karthāgō Karthāginis f.: Carthage (4)

— L —

Labeō Labeōnis m.: Labeo (1)

labor labōris m.: toil, exertion (1)

Lacedaemōn Lacedaemonis f.: Sparta

Lacedaemonius –a –um: Spartan, Lacedaemonian (1)

laus laudis f.: praise, glory

lectīca –ae f.: litter (1)

lēgātus –ī m.: lieutenant, envoy (6)

legō legere lēgī lēctus: gather; choose; read

levis leve: light, trivial

libēns libentis: gladly, happily, willing (1)

liber –ī m.: book (2)

Ligurēs Ligurum m.: Ligurians (a people in the north–west coast of Italy) (1)

littera –ae f.: letter; (pl.) literature (2)

lītus lītoris n.: shore (1)

locus –ī m.: place; **loca:** (n. pl.) region (6)

longus –ī m.: Longus (1)

Longus –a –um: long, prolonged (1)

Lūcānī –ōrum m.: Lucanians, the region of Lucania in southern Italy (6)

Lucius –ī m.: Lucius (4)

— M —

magis: more, in a higher degree (1)

magister magistrī m.: master, chief (1)

magistrātus magistrātūs m.: magistrate (2)

magnitūdō magnitūdinis f.: greatness, bulk

magnus –a –um: great (6)

Māgo Māgōnis m.: Mago (brother of Hannibal) (5)

maiōrēs maiōrum m.: ancestors

Manlius –ī m.: Manlius (1)

manus manūs f.: hand; band of men (2)

Marcellus –ī m.: Marcellus (2)

Marcus –ī m.: Marcus (6)

mare maris n.: sea (3)

māter mātris f.: mother

mātrimōnium –ī n.: marriage, matrimony

Māximus –ī m.: Maximus (1)

memor memoris: mindful (+gen.) (1)

memoria –ae f.: recollection, memory (2)

mēns mentis f.: mind, heart (1)

mentiō mentiōnis f.: mention (2)

mercēs mercēdis f.: pay, wages

meus –a –um: my (1)

mīles mīlitis m.: soldier (1)

mīlle mīlia: thousand (1)

Minucius –ī m.: Minucius (2)

mīror mīrārī mīrātus sum: wonder at, marvel at (+acc.) (1)

mittō mittere mīsī missum: send, let go (5)

modus –ī m.: measure, manner, kind (2)

mōns montis m.: mountain (1)

morbus –ī m.: sickness, disease (1)

moror morārī morātus sum: delay (1)

mortuus –a –um: dead (1)

mōs mōris m.: custom, habit; character (in pl.)

multitūdō –inis f.: multitude, number (6)

multus –a –um: much, many; multō, by far (8)

mūniō mūnīre mūnīvī mūnītum: build (1)

mūnus mūneris n.: gift, offering; duty, obligation; (pl.) gladiatorial show (2)

mūsica –ae f.: music

— N —

nam or namque: for, indeed, really (7)

nāscor nāscī nātus sum: be born (2)

nātiō nātiōnis f.: people, nation, race (2)

naufragium –ī n.: shipwreck (1)

nauticus –a –um: naval (1)

nāvālis nāvāle: naval (1)

nāvis nāvis f.: ship (13)

nē: lest, that not (7)

negō –āre: deny, refuse (1)

nēmō nēminis: no one (gen. nūllīus, dat. nūllī, abl. nūllō or nūllā) (8)

neque: and not, nor; **nec...nec:** neither...nor (7)

nihil: nothing; not at all (3)

nisi: if not, unless (5)

nōbilis nōbile: distinguished, noble; a nobleman or woman (as subst.)

noctū: by night (1)

nōmen nōminis n.: name (1)

nōn: not (19)

noster nostra nostrum: our

novem: nine (1)

novus –a –um: new (3)

nox noctis f.: night (2)

nūllus –a –um: no one, not any (2)

num: interrogative particle implying negative answer (1)

Numida –ae m.: Numidian (a tribe in northern Africa) (1)

numquam: never (4)

nunc: now (1)

nūntiō -āre: report (1)

ob: against, on account of (+acc.) (1)

obdūcō -dūcere -dūxī -ductum: envelop, overspread (1)

— O —

obiciō -icere -iēcī -iectum: oppose, set against (2)

obitus obitūs m.: death (1)

obses obsidis m./f.: hostages (2)

obsideō -sidēre -sēdī -sessum: besiege (1)

obtrectātiō obtrectātiōnis f.: detraction, disparagement (1)

obviam: against (1)

occīdō -cīdere -cīdī -cīsum: kill, cut down (1)

occupō -āre: seize, occupy; anticipate, do a thing first (+infin.) (3)

oculus -ī m.: eye (1)

odium -ī n.: hatred (2)

Olympia -ae f.: Olympia

omittō -mittere -mīsī -missum: neglect, omit (1)

omnis omne: all, every, as a whole (13)

opera -ae f.: labor, activity, work (2)

operiō operīre operuī opertum: cover over (1)

oppleō -plēre -plēvī -plētum: fill up (1)

opprimō -primere -pressī -pressum: crush, overpower (2)

ops opis f.: assistance, resources (2)

optimus -a -um: best, excellent; adv. **optimē** (1)

ōrnātus -a -um: equipped, furnished (1)

ostendō ostendere ostendī ostentum: show, hold out (2)

— P —

Padus -ī m.: Padus River (major river in northern Italy; modern Po) (2)

palam: openly (2)

Pamphȳlius -a -um: of Pamphylia (region in southern Asia Minor) (1)

pār paris: equal (5)

pāreō pārēre pāruī: obey (1)

parō -āre: make, prepare, provide (1)

pars partis f.: part (1)

partim: partly, in part

parvus -a -um: small (1)

passus passūs m.: step, pace or five feet (1)

patefaciō -facere -fēcī -factum: lay open (1)

pater patris m.: father, ancestor (4)

paternus -a -um: fatherly, paternal (1)

patior patī passus sum: permit, endure (1)

patria -ae f.: fatherland, country (3)

paucī -ae -a: few (5)

Paulus -ī m.: Paulus (2)

pāx pācis f.: peace (2)

pecūnia -ae f.: money (3)

pedester pedestris pedestre: on foot, on land, of infantry (1)

pellō pellere pepulī pulsum: strike, beat, push, drive (4)

pendō pendere pependī pēnsum: weigh, hang, suspend; pay (1)

per: through (+acc.) (1)

perfugiō -fugere -fūgī: flee (1)

perfungor -fungī -fūnctus sum: perform, endure (1)

Pergamēnus -a -um: of Pergamum (a kingdom in Asia Minor) (3) perīculum -ī n.: danger (1)

persequor -sequī -secūtus sum: follow, pursue

persōna -ae f.: role, character

persuādeō -suādēre -suāsī -suāsum: persuade (1)

perterreō -terrēre -terruī -territum: terrify (1)

pertineō -tinēre -tinuī: extend over, reach; refer to, pertain to, be the business of (1)

perveniō -venīre -vēnī -ventum: arrive, reach (6)

petō petere petīvī petītum: seek, aim at (6)

Philippus -ī m.: Philip (V, king of Macedon) (1)

plērusque plēraque plērumque: the greater part, very many, most, the majority; plērumque: generally

plumbum -ī n.: lead (1)

plūrimus -a -um: the greatest number of, very many; plūrimī: most people (1)

plūs plūris: a greater amount or number, more (2)

poena -ae f.: penalty, punishment (1)

Poenus -ī m.: Phoenician, Carthaginian (3)

polliceor -licērī -licitus sum: promise (1)

Polybius -ī m.: Polybius (1)

pōnō pōnere posuī positum: put, place; put aside (2)

Pontus -ī m.: Pontus (kingdom in northeastern Asia Minor) (1)

populus -ī m.: people (3)

portō -āre: carry a load (2)

possum posse potuī: be able (10)

post: after (adv. and prep. +acc.) (6)

posteā: afterwards (3)

posteāquam: after (1)

posterus –a –um: next, later (1)

postquam: after (3)

postulō –āre: ask for, demand, require (2)

potēns potentis: able, powerful (1)

potestās potestātis f.: power (1)

potissimum: first of all, especially, principally (1)

praebeō praebēre praebuī praebitum: furnish, supply, render (1)

praecipiō –cipere –cēpī –ceptum: anticipate, advise, warn (2)

praeferō –ferre –tulī –lātum: prefer (1)

praemium –ī n.: bounty, reward (1)

praesēns praesentis: present, in person, ready (1)

praesidium –ī n.: garrison, protection (1)

praestō –stāre –stitī –stitum: excel, exhibit (1)

praesum –esse –fuī: preside or take charge of (+dat.) (3)

praeter: by, along, past; besides, except (+acc.) (2)

praetereā: besides, moreover (1)

praetor praetōris m.: praetor, one of the chief Roman magistrates (2)

praetūra –ae f.: praetorship (1)

premō premere pressī pressum: press, pursue, overwhelm (2)

prīmus –a –um: first; adv. **prīmum:** at first, firstly (1)

prīnceps prīncipis: first, chief (2)

prior prius: earlier, preceding; **prius** or **priusquam:** before (1)

prīstinus –a –um: former (1)

priusquam: before (2)

prōdeō –īre –ivī –itum: appear in public, exhibit, go/come forward

prōdō –dere –didī –ditum: publish, hand down; give over, betray (2)

prōdūcō –dūcere –dūxī –ductum: lead forth (1)

proelium -ī n.: battle (6)

proficīscor -ficīscī -fectus sum: set forth, go (5)

profiteor -fitērī -fessus sum: declare publicly (1)

proflīgō -āre: overwhelm, crush, defeat decisively (1)

profugiō -fugere -fūgī: flee (1)

prohibeō -hibēre -hibuī -hibitum: restrain, keep away (1)

prōpatulum -ī n.: open courtyard (1)

prope: near, next, (comp.) **propior,** (superl.) **proximus;** (adv.) **prope:** nearly, almost (1)

properē: quickly (1)

propinquus -a -um: near, neighboring (+dat.) (1)

prōpōnō -pōnere -posuī -positum: put forth, propose, present

propter: because of (+acc.) (2)

prōspiciō -spicere -spēxī -spectum: look out (1)

prōvideō -vidēre -vīdī -vīsum: prepare, make ready (1)

proximus -a -um: next, nearest (2)

prūdentia -ae f.: practical skill, intelligence (2)

Prūsias -ae m.: Prusias (king of Bithynia) (4)

pūblicō -āre: confiscate (1)

pūblicus -a -um: public, belonging to the state (1)

Publius -ī m.: Publius (4)

pudeō pudēre puduī puditus: be ashamed, make ashamed

puer puerī m.: boy; slave (2)

puerulus -ī m.: little boy (1)

pugna -ae f.: fist-fight; battle (3)

pugnō -āre: fight (3)

puppis puppis f.: ship, stern (1)

putō –āre: think, suppose

Pȳrēnaeus –a –um: of the Pyrenees (mountain range between Hispania and Gaul) (1)

– Q –

quaerō quaerere quaesīvī quaesītum: seek, inquire (2)

quam: how? (after comparative) than (6)

quamdiū: as long as (1)

quantus –a –um: (interr.) how great? (rel.) of what size, amount, etc. (2)

quārē: how? why? (1)

que: and (enclitic) (34)

quī quae quod (rel. pronoun): who, which, what (83)

quī quae quod (interrogative adj.): who, which, what (70)

quisquam quicquam/quidquam: any (single) person, anyone at all (1)

quīcumque quaecumque quodcumque: whoever, whatever (1)

quidem: certainly, at least (2)

quīn: indeed, in fact; (conj.) so that...not (+subj.) (2)

Quinctius –ī m.: Quinctius (1)

quīnque: five (2)

quīnquiēns: five times (1)

Quintus –ī m.: Quintus (3)

quippe: indeed, surely

quis quid: (interrogative adj.) who? what? (4)

quō: for which reason; to or in what place; to what end, for what purpose? (3)

quod: because (4)

quoque: also, too (4)

quotannīs: every year (1)

quotiēnscumque: how often, as often as (1)

Full Vocabulary 149

— R —

ratiō ratiōnis f.: method, plan, reason (1)

recipiō –cipere –cēpī –ceptum: take back, receive; **sē recipere:** betake oneself, go (2)

rēctus –a –um: straight, direct

recūsō –āre: protest (1)

reddō –dere –didī –ditum: return, give back (3)

redeō –īre –iī –itum: go back, return (3)

referō referre rettulī relātum: bring back; report (1)

rēgnum –ī n.: kingship, kingdom (1)

relinquō –linquere –līquī –lictum: abandon (4)

reliquus –a –um: left, left over, remaining (3)

remittō –mittere –mīsī –missum: send back (1)

removeō –movēre –mōvī –mōtum: remove, dismiss (2)

renūntiō –āre: report (1)

reor rērī rātus sum: think, imagine, suppose, deem (1)

repente: suddenly (1)

repentīnō: suddenly (1)

reperiō reperīre repperī repertum: find, find out (2)

rēpō rēpere rēpsī rēptum: crawl (1)

repōnō –pōnere –posuī –positum: place, deposit (1)

rēs reī f.: matter, affair, situation (13)

rēscīscō –scīscere –scīvī –scītum: find out, get to know (1)

resistō –stere –stitī: resist, oppose (2)

respōnsum –ī n.: response, reply (2)

retineō –tinēre –tinuī –tentum: hold back, keep (1)

revertō –vertere –vertī: turn back (1)

revocō –āre: call back, recall (2)

rēx rēgis m.: king (14)

Rhodanus –ī m.: Rhodanus River (major river in southern Gaul; modern Rhône) (2)

Rhodius –a –um: of Rhodes (island in eastern Mediterranean) (2)

rīdeō rīdēre rīsī rīsum: laugh, laugh at (1)

rōbustus –a –um: strong (1)

rogō –āre: ask (1)

Rōma –ae f.: Rome (5)

Rōmānus –a –um: Roman (20)

ruber rubra rubrum: red (1)

Rūfus –ī m.: Rufus (1)

– S –

sacrificō –āre: make sacrifice, sacrifice (1)

saepe: often (1)

Saguntum –ī n.: Saguntum (town in eastern Spain) (1)

saltō –āre: dance

saltus saltūs m.: mountain pass (3)

salūs salūtis f.: health, safety (1)

sarmentum –ī n.: twig, branch (1)

satis/sat: enough, sufficiently (2)

saucius –a –um: wounded (1)

scaena –ae f.: stage (of a theater)

scapha –ae f.: small boat, skiff (1)

scīlicet: certainly, of course (1)

sciēns scientis: skilled, expert

sciō scīre scīvī/–iī scītum: know (1)

Scīpiō Scīpiōnis m.: Scipio (4)

scrībō scrībere scrīpsī scrīptum: write (3)

scrīptūra –ae f.: writing, composition

secundus –a –um: following; favorable (1)

sed: but (8)

sedeō sedēre sēdī sessum: sit

sēgregō –āre: separate, exclude, remove (1)

sēiungō –iungere –iūnxī –iūnctus: separate (1)

semper: always, ever (2)

Semprōnius –ī m.: Sempronius (1)

senātus senātūs m.: senate (4)

sentiō sentīre sēnsī sēnsum: perceive, feel, hear, see (2)

septuāgēsimus –a –um: seventieth (1)

sequor sequī secūtus sum: follow

sermō sermōnis m.: conversation, discourse (1)

serpēns serpentis f.: snake (3)

Servīlius –ī m.: Servilius (1)

servulus –ī m.: young slave (1)

sētius: less, in a lesser degree (1)

sī: if (12)

sīc: in this manner, thus; **sīc...ut:** in the same way as (7)

signum –ī n.: sign, standard, mark (1)

Sīlēnus –ī m.: Silenus (1)

simul: at the same time (4)

simulō –āre: pretend, put on the appearance of (1)

sine: without (+abl.) (3)

societās societātis f.: alliance (1)

sōlum: only, merely (3)

solvō solvere solvī solūtum: release, set sail (2)

soror sorōris f.: sister

Sōsylus -ī m.: Sosylus (2)

spectāculum -ī n.: show, sight, spectacle

spēs speī f.: hope (1)

statim: immediately (2)

statua -ae f.: statue (1)

stultus -a -um: foolish (1)

subigō -igere -ēgī -āctus: conquer, subdue (1)

sufficiō -ficere -fēcī -fectus: appoint to a magistracy in place of another (1)

sui sibi sē sē/sēsē: himself, herself, itself (30)

Sulpicius -ī m.: Sulpicius (2)

sum esse fuī futūrus: be, exist, live (61)

summus -a -um: highest, farthest, last (3)

sūmō sūmere sūmpsī sūmptum: take up (1)

superō -āre: overcome, surpass, defeat (5)

supersum -esse -fuī: remain, survive; be superfluous (to) (1)

superus -a -um: situated above, upper; **superī -ōrum m. pl.:** those above, i.e., the gods (3)

suprā: above, beyond (adv. and prep. +acc.) (1)

suscipiō -cipere -cēpī -ceptus: take up (2)

sustineō sustinēre sustinuī sustentum: hold up, sustain (1)

suus -a -um: his own, her own, its own (13)

Syria -ae f.: Syria (2)

— T —

tabellārius tabellāriī m.: letter-carrier, messenger (2)

tālis tāle: such (4)

tam: so, so much (1)

tamen: nevertheless, still (2)

Tamphilus –ī m.: Tamphilus (2)

tamquam: so as, just as (1)

tantus –a –um: so great, so much; **tantum / tantummodo:** only (6)

templum –ī n.: consecrated ground; temple (2)

tempus temporis n.: time (5)

teneō tenēre tenuī tentum: have, keep (2)

Terentius –ī m.: Terentius (1)

terra –ae f.: land (1)

terror terrōris m.: terror (1)

tertius –a –um: third (4)

Thermopylae –ārum f.: Thermopylae (1)

Tiberis Tiberis m./f.: Tiber River (1)

Tiberius –ī m.: Tiberius (2)

tībia –ae f.: reed–pipe

Titus –ī m.: Titus (1)

tollō tollere sustulī sublātum: raise up, destroy (2)

tōtus –a –um: whole, entire

trādūcō –dūcere –dūxī –ductum: lead across (1)

trānseō trānsīre trānsiī trānsitum: go across (4)

Trasumēnus –ī m.: Trasimene (lake in Etruria) (1)

Trebia –ae f.: Trebia (river in Cisalpine Gaul) (2)

trecentī –ae –a: three hundred (1)

trēs tria: three (1)

tribuō tribuere tribuī tribūtum: assign, grant (1)

triennium –ī n.: three year period (1)

tū tuī tibi tē tē: you (1)

tum: then (3)

turpis turpe: ugly

turpitūdō turpitūdinis f.: shamefulness, disgrace

— U —

ubi: where, when (3)

ūllus −a −um: any, anyone (1)

umquam: ever (1)

unde: from where (1)

undique: from all sides, on all sides (1)

ūniversus −a −um: all together (1)

ūnus −a −um: one (8)

urbs urbis f.: city (1)

ūsque: up to; continuously (3)

ūsus ūsūs m.: use, experience (1)

ut: as (+indic.); so that, with the result that (+subj.) (20)

uterque utraque utrumque: each of two (4)

ūtor ūtī ūsus sum: use, employ, apply (+abl.) (2)

utpote: namely (reinforcing an explanation) (1)

utrobīque: on both sides (1)

uxor uxōris f.: wife

— V —

valēns valentis: strong, powerful (1)

valeō valēre valuī: be strong, excel, be valid, prevail; **valē:** farewell! (1)

valētūdō valētūdinis f.: health; illness (1)

vāllum −ī n.: rampart; protection (1)

varius −a −um: changing, varied, various (1)

vāsum -ī n.: vase, container (2)

vectīgal vectīgālis n.: tax, levy (1)

vehō vehere vēxī vectum: carry; **vehor vehī vectus sum:** travel, ride (1)

vēlum -ī n.: sail (1)

velut: even as, just as (1)

venēnō -āre: poison (1)

venēnum -ī n.: poison (1)

veniō venīre vēnī ventum: come (9)

ventus -ī m.: wind (1)

Venusia -ae f.: Venusia (town in southern Italy) (1)

verbum -ī n.: word (1)

vereor verērī veritus sum: fear, stand in awe of (2)

vērō: in fact, certainly, without doubt

versō -āre: come and go frequently, move, turn

vertō vertere vertī versum: turn (1)

vērus -a -um: true (1)

vīcēsimus -a -um: twentieth (1)

victor victōris m.: conqueror, victor

videō vidēre vīdī vīsum: see (6)

vidua -ae f.: widow, unmarried woman

vīgintī: twenty (1)

vincō vincere vīcī victum: conquer (1)

vir virī m.: man (5)

virtūs virtūtis f.: valor, manliness, virtue (3)

vīs, vīs f.: force; (acc.) **vim** (abl.), **vī** (pl.); **vīrēs:** strength (2)

vīsus vīsūs m.: sight, appearance, vision (1)

vīta vītae f.: life (1)

vītō –āre: avoid, shun (1)

vīvō vīvere vīxī vīctum: live (1)

vīvus –a –um: alive, living (2)

vix: scarcely (1)

volō velle voluī: wish, be willing (2)

Volsō Volsōnis m.: Volso (1)

volūmen volūminis n.: book, volume

voluntās voluntātis f.: wish, desire (1)

– Z –

Zama –ae f.: Zama (town southwest of Carthage) (2)

This book need not end here...

At Open Book Publishers, we are changing the nature of the traditional academic book. The title you have just read will not be left on a library shelf, but will be accessed online by hundreds of readers each month across the globe. We make all our books free to read online so that students, researchers and members of the public who can't afford a printed edition can still have access to the same ideas as you.

Our digital publishing model also allows us to produce online supplementary material, including extra chapters, reviews, links and other digital resources. Find *Cornelius Nepos, 'Life of Hannibal'* on our website to access its online extras. Please check this page regularly for ongoing updates, and join the conversation by leaving your own comments:

http://www.openbookpublishers.com/isbn/9781783741328

If you enjoyed this book, and feel that research like this should be available to all readers, regardless of their income, please think about donating to us. Our company is run entirely by academics, and our publishing decisions are based on intellectual merit and public value rather than on commercial viability. We do not operate for profit and all donations, as with all other revenue we generate, will be used to finance new Open Access publications.

For further information about what we do, how to donate to OBP, additional digital material related to our titles or to order our books, please visit our website: http://www.openbookpublishers.com